The Prisoner of Sex

Also by Norman Mailer

The Prisoner of Sex

Norman Mailer

DONALD I. FINE, INC.

New York

LIBRARY OF CONGRESS CATALOGUE CARD NUMBER: 85-80630
ISBN: 0-917657-59-4
MANUFACTURED IN THE UNITED STATES OF AMERICA
10 9 8 7 6 5 4 3 2 1

To Carol Stevens

INTRODUCTION
by
PETE HAMILL

To read this wonderfully amusing book again, fifteen years after its composition, is to be reminded again of the differences between battle reports and history. It would be impossible, of course, to write a full history of the American Sixties (that lumpy bag of a decade that began in Dallas on November 22, 1963 and ended with the fall of Saigon twelve years later) without consulting, absorbing and understanding the journalism of Norman Mailer. He seemed to be everywhere in those years, intuitively knowing that the decade's story was not only on the battlefields of Indochina, but among the people and places that had been disrupted, ennobled or degraded in the multiple upheavals that evolved from the war. He filed his reports from political conventions, prizefights, demonstrations; he took note of voyages to the moon; he ran for Mayor of New York. Honors fell upon him; television gave him an immensely wide audience, the kind of fame that could be glibly dismissed as mere celebrity if it were not for the extraordinary quality of his work.

But Mailer would probably be the first to agree that his finest work of the era (excepting *An American Dream*, one of his best novels) took the form of urgent bulletins, as incomplete as any journalism, subject to all the flaws of judgment that come with haste. He brought to those reports a novelist's eye, ear and sense of design; he added the imaginative intelligence of a modern man, shaped by the intellectual currents that flowed through New York from Europe (and elsewhere) in the years after World War Two. If his own public voice was first heard in 1957 in his essay *The White*

Negro, he expanded, refined, deepened that voice throughout the Sixties. He made journalism that was literature in his communiques from the front; history must be left to duller men.

The voice was, to be sure, egocentric; Mailer was not the first writer to be more interested in his own reactions to events than he was to the unfolding story. And yet the work in retrospect seems remarkably free of empty vanity. The strategy of placing himself at the center of the story might have been Mailer's own form of Sixties protest, because at the feverish height of the era, crowds seemed to have forced individuals off the stage of history. Mailer might agree with the position of a group, even join an occasional committee; but when he entered the bazaar, he always offered his own wares, guaranteed to be made by hand. Part of him was a pitchman, of course, forever advertising himself, but he was saved from the pomposity of the blind narcissist by his refined hard New York sense of irony; nobody saw Mailer's occasional stupidities more clearly (or affectionately) than Mailer. And they too were included in the reports.

This book is one of those reports. When it was published, a number of feminists attacked it or dismissed it as blatant reactionary male chauvinism. And although Mailer is, in some crucial ways, a profoundly conservative man, his targets in this essay are not women or feminism, but dishonesty, inhumane technology and cant.

The opening section is jolly self-revelation, as Mailer recounts some of his feelings after the break-up of his fourth marriage and his attempts to cope with his five young children during a long vacation in Maine. He is at this point in his late forties, a scarred but undefeated veteran of numerous wars, foreign and domestic; his long book about the moon landing has been finished; there is a sense of things burned out in the man. But the tone contains no self-pity, no adolescent whine; he is even relieved when he learns that he has not won the Nobel Prize that year. Somehow, he copes with the children, and is happy. But that is the summer of Women's Liberation. He is asked to discuss the subject for a *Time* cover story, mulls this offer, decides against it, then learns that the feminists consider him, in the *Time* editor's phrase, "their major ideological opposition."

Mailer writes, "Now he was tempted. To be the center of any situation was, he sometimes thought, the real marrow of his bone—better to expire as a devil in the fire than an angel in the wings."

He decides against the *Time* cover, but broods about

his reputation among the feminists. "It was hard to think of himself as one of their leading enemies," he writes. "Four times beaten at wedlock, his respect for the power of women was so large that the way they would tear through him (in his mind's eye) would be reminiscent of old newsreels of German tanks crunching through straw huts on their way across a border."

But he hears talk about a book by Kate Millet called *Sexual Politics*; he reads snotty references to himself in another feminist book; he recalls unsettling encounters with Gloria Steinem and Bella Abzug, and then . . . Millet ends up on the cover of *Time*! These were obviously all signs and portents, and Mailer realizes he must write something about women and their liberation.

". . . The themes of his life had gathered here. Revolution, tradition, sex and the homosexual, the orgasm, the family, the child and the political shape of the future, technology and human conception, waste and abortion, the ethics of the critic and the male mystique, black rights and new thoughts on women's rights—the themes were pervasive enough to depress him."

And off he goes. The result was this book. It is not reportage; it is analysis, in the long, honorable tradition of the pamphlet, and I don't intend to vulgarize

Mailer's ideas by attempting to summarize them here. As they say in the Carnegie Deli, better you should read the book.

But I do think the new reader should pay attention to Mailer's method. In a way, this is a book about the processes of Mailer's thinking, and it offers a wonderful example of the difference between the artist and the academic. Hidden in the academy, the dull scribe piles up facts, presents thesis and antithesis, hedges his bets, and publishes for his fellow academics. But most artists are in some critical way performers; they might want to change the world, seduce its inhabitants, accrue honors, fame and money; but essentially they are showing off. The showoff says: Look, I am here, I exist, I am different, look what I can do. The size of the audience doesn't really matter. And Mailer in all of his work is giving us a performance.

He is not, however, the kind of performer who works from other people's scripts, and rereading this book, I was reminded again that the most interesting artists of Mailer's young manhood were not writers, but musicians. If Charlie Parker or John Coltrane had been writers, they'd have gone at their tasks the way Mailer does. Again and again, Mailer enters his piece with a light-hearted prologue, then states the melody or theme. From there he races off on an improvisation whose brilliance and complexity are up to him on any given evening, free of the constraints of conventional form, able to call on as much of what he knows (about the world, the self) as he cares to reveal. I suspect that Mailer is often as surprised by his sudden twists and turns, his showering choruses of ideas and words and sounds, as a great bebop musician is. In this book, the growing excitement of his exploration is obvious. The prose races; there are sentences that run on and on, in Faulknerian cadences, as if Mailer sensed that if he stopped, paused for breath, opened his eyes and looked at the faces in Birdland, he would lose it all.

In *The White Negro*, Mailer wrote that the black man's music "gave voice to the character and quality of his existence, to his rage and the infinite variations of joy, lust, languor, growl, cramp, pinch, scream and despair of his orgasm. For jazz is orgasm, it is the music of orgasm, good orgasm and bad, and so it spoke across a nation, it had the communication of art even where it was watered, perverted, corrupted, and almost killed, it spoke in no matter what laundered popular way of instantaneous existential states to which some whites could respond, it was indeed a communication by art because it said, 'I feel this, and now you do too.' "

That seems to me to be at the heart of Mailer's journalistic ambition: he feels this, and he wants us to feel it too. And he has absorbed one other lesson from jazz: the parallel of its structures to fucking. The best of his journalism has the coiled tension, intricate variations, explosive release of a great fuck. So does a tune played by a great jazz musician. The structures of novels are different; the designs are grander, more European, closer to symphonies or extravagant murals (Charlie Parker was essentially a dazzlingly original draftsman, as are the best journalists). When the Sixties were over, and Mailer moved back to the novel, he gave us *Ancient Evenings*, a dense original opaque symphony, not a slow blues on a Saturday night.

Read this book, and you will follow Mailer as he moves from peak to peak of the performance, his tone alternately self-mocking, scathing, mystical, angry, serene. Sometimes the form is call-and-response. Sometimes it is solo mockery. He raises huge cosmic questions on some pages, and throws a guildsman's hug around the shoulders of Henry Miller on others. Mailer the novelist enjoys conflict, the bruising essence of drama; Mailer the philosopher ponders the meaning of existence in a single sperm; Mailer the hornplayer holds all of it together with the skills of the virtuoso. Quarrel with the player, attack his premises, sneer at his inventions if you will. But I, for one, am glad he made a record of the performance and that once again we can place it on a turntable and listen.

The
Prisoner
of Sex

I The Prizewinner

EAR THE END of the Year of the Polymor-
phous Perverse (which is to say in the
fall of '69) there were rumors he would
win the Nobel. Then a perfect flurry. An
inquiry from the New York office of UPI.

3

Would he cooperate to the extent of keeping them right up on his whereabouts for the next full day? "Find out why," he said. His secretary had not been working for him long, and they were still unattuned to each other's taste. "Yes, I'll tell him," she murmured into the phone, and looked up with eyes so rich in admiration she could have been confronting the Honorable Ex-Supreme Court Justice Arthur J. Goldberg. "The word from Stockholm is that you're going to get the Nobel Prize."

"It's impossible," he said. After twenty-one years of public life he had the equivalent of a Geiger counter in his brain to measure the radiation of advancements and awards in the various salients, wedges, and vectors of that aesthetic battlefield known as the literary pie.

"Well, talk to him," she said.

One of those hard scraped wire-service voices with a Scotch-Irish name was at the other end. "We've reason to believe it's going to be announced in the next few hours, and we would appreciate being able to reach you then."

They could, he countered, call his secretary at the number just used, for she would be in touch with him. And hung up feeling nothing at all remarkable.

"Aren't you excited?" she asked.

"No."

"You amaze me."

"I'm not going to get it, for one thing. There's been some mistake. For another . . ."

The truth was that he was not absolutely certain. Half a year ago, on that spring day he had been awarded the Pulitzer Prize, advance notice had come via a *New York Times* man. It was therefore possible the news was accurate again. Even so, he would not want the Nobel. Not this year. It was a season of large and little deaths for ten thousand seedlings of the psyche. His wife and he had parted this summer — his fourth wife! — split after near to seven years. A considerable part of him had been used up and used up again in relocating his soul. Yet after a marriage had gone to the guillotine, the deaths in oneself were small compared to the loss one sensed of all those delightful potentialities in the children which depended on the taking together of the daily bread. Sorrow lay its protection over him like a shawl on the bones of an arthritic. What monstrous timing it would be to win a prize now and smile one's mouth out over a choppy sea of congratulations. But then if his life presented any pattern, it was of just such monstrous and maladroit timing. By that logic, he would be certain to add FNPW to his name this afternoon. Not Vladimir Nabokov, Famous Nobel Prize Winner; not Robert Lowell, FNPW; not Saul Bellow nor Malamud nor Günter

5

Grass nor Yokio Mishima nor Jean Genet. Not — he knew three or four huge literary names were eluding him at the moment. Indeed, it would be an embarrassment to win. How could one really look Nabokov in the eye? Or Henry Miller?

All day the phone was ringing. People had heard on television that he was up for the prize. All day he was calm. No, he would tell them, he was not about to win. In fact — he did not say this aloud — he really did not care. In fact, he suspected it might bother him. After all, he felt no intimation that the wings of any award were hovering near, and his ability to apprehend what lived on the other side of the hill was more valuable to him than a medal. (Especially since he could not see across a room.)

By evening arrived the true report. Samuel Beckett had been given the prize over André Malraux. One had to be a hint illiterate not to have thought of either name. Let us hope modesty prevented him from considering his own work for even an instant in comparison; Malraux, after all, was his idea of a great writer.

Humor followed. "The word from Stockholm!" You could bet your fiery ass. Somebody in news service, wire service, or television at your service, had never heard Malraux's name before and so decided it was a Swedish misspelling of his own. Doubtless.

Afterward, he was pleased at his indifference during that long day. What a wound the award would have left if he had coveted the fame. But indeed he hadn't. Fame — even the limited measure of it thrust on him — was no more than a strange face holding a microphone in your own face, and asking questions one had answered a hundred times before. "What do you think of the political situation in New York today?" (Most of the questions came from philosophical deserts the Media had left behind while washing and scouring the great collective brain.) Fame was your phone ringing a few times more each week to request interviews you did not wish to give and didn't, fame was people with kindly intentions interrupting your thoughts on the street, fame was the inhibition which kept you from taking a piss in a strange alley for fear of cops and headlines on a front page, fame kept you from making a fool of yourself on the dance floor. Fame was the inability to get boozed anonymously in a strange bar, which meant it was the inability to nurse an obsessive melancholy through a night of revelations. That was fame of a minor order. But the Nobel Prize would have incarcerated him into larger paralyses. Each time there was a change of government in Canberra or Pakistan, some poor reporter would have his name on a list of notables to be called for a statement. Committees and charity dinners, satellite awards and subsidiary distinctions would have an outsize lust to list him. Fame — by existential measure — could only increase the nugatory quotient of one's deeds. Fame would then be saying no to more people, and spending time with people one would not otherwise go near. Fame, unless one had a mission, was equal to the taste of aspirin in one's death, and he had no mission this year. He thought with relief of all the literary envies which had not been sparked among his friends and enemies by being given so half-respected and half-cherished a prize before he was old enough, deserving, or ready. And in his larger gloom, he again found time to be pleased at caring so little that he would not wear FNPW after his name. Yet the initials teased for employment. Why should they not? He had spent an absurd day with them. As a reminder, he let them stand for False Nobel Prize Winner. Was FNPW finally growing up to discover the size or real lack of size of His Talent? After a while it was natural to use the shortened form. Squire Writer, PW. Hardy Husband, PW.

Since PW could also stand for Prisoner of War (which he could amend to Prisoner of Wedlock, for he had never been able to live without a woman) he had another name for himself, the PW, Prisoner or Prizewinner? They were polar concepts to be regarded at opposite ends of his ego — so they provided a base for his reactions whenever that equivalent of a phallus, that ghost-phallus of the mentality, firm strong-tongued ego, had wandered onto unfamiliar scenes. After a time he thought of himself often as the Prisoner. He did not know why, nor what he was prisoner of. It was simply that his ego did not rise very often these days to the emoluments of the Prizewinner. His mood was nearer to the dungeon. For his battered not-so-firm ego was obliged to be installed in Provincetown through a long winter to go through the double haul of writing a book about the first landing on the moon while remaking himself out of the loss of a fourth wife. It was a winter to offer all the excitement which comes from dredging the liver. He spent cold months of meditation on the rivets that hold a rocket together, and in the late spring of '70, time of deliverance, his long work was done, he went up to Maine with five of his six children (the oldest would be in Europe for the summer) determined to get some idea of what it might be like to raise a family, for it was on this point that his last marriage had begun to wallow, then had sunk: his fourth wife, an actress, had seen her career drown in the rigors of managing so large a home.

If the Prisoner had commenced with the idea that he would have no maids and no personal life for the six weeks he would be with the children, that he and the girls, thirteen, ten, and eight, would do the shopping, cooking, and cleaning, and care for the boys, six and four, that was amended quickly. A good Maine woman, familiar with the house he rented and looking for work, was available, so she did the cleaning and laundry, which turned out to be a full task, and his sister came up to help him for two weeks, and then an old love, his dearest old love, was invited up once, and filling some critical abyss in the well-concealed hole of his heart was invited up again for the rest of the summer. Now they alternated duty days in the kitchen. He did not think he had necessarily abrogated any true contract with himself. There was always work with five children, and his wife, after all, had never been without help for long. So, short of some nonexistent urge toward the Spartan or regurgitated karma from the Essene, there was nothing to demand that he not only take care of the kids, but live altogether removed from velvet, chocolate, and sex. In a Maine ménage, which must have excited some remarkable curiosity from the exterior but was close to reasonable within, he therefore spent six good hardworking mindless weeks with his daughters, his sons, and his mistress, his brain full of menus and shopping lists and projects and outings. Rainy days arrived like examinations for which one was not prepared after clear days out of doors when the boys rollicked like otters in the Maine hills and dreamed of the year they could sail their own brig. They were obviously small powers out of doors. Inside, on rainy afternoons, their whining gave a hint of the whistle in the pipes of a maniac. Still, his daughters often delivered arts on those rainy days to entertain his sons. He had always been proud of his daughters, yet in these six weeks he mounted into such vertigoes of paternal pride as to come to the conclusion they were deserving of an accolade. They were sensational. They did their chores and helped the boys to dress and go to bed, aided with the cooking and the dishes and the pots and with the wire perambulators in the shopping marts. And were happy. Happy. It was not an unhappy summer, and he ended with the knowledge that he could run a decent home and sleep without a turn of guilt, knew he could run a home without screaming at children and be as a result thus mind-empty at night that solitaire pleased him, knew he could immerse himself in the unintriguing subtleties of the thousand acts of order and timing which made the difference between efficient and catastrophic keeping of house — could do all this for year after year and never write another word, be content, honorably fatigued, empty of doubt about his worth, free of dread, all credit deposited to his moral foundations, but in no uncertainty that the most interesting part of his mind and heart was condemned to dry on the vine. Yes, he could be a housewife for six weeks, even for six years if it came to it, even work without help if it came to it, but he did not question what he would have to give up forever. So he could not know whether he would have found it endurable to be born a woman or if it would have driven him out onto the drear avenues of the insane.

The question therefore was not so much answered as honored by his summer experiment; his ego, at least, was rested. The Prisoner had not contemplated his ego in weeks. He did not have to when his dungarees were dank with the water of pots and he knew at last what a woman meant when she said her hair smelled of grease. In fact, he now possessed an operative definition of remarkable banalities. "The children almost drove me mad" was rich in context to him, and he could hardly have done without the lament of the truly wasted, "I didn't have a thought to myself all day." They were clichés. They were also paving blocks at the crossroads of existence. Who could deny after an experience like his own that all the big questions might just as well originate here.

2

While the Prizewinner was packing lunches this picnicking summer, the particular part of his ghost-phallus which remained in New York — his very reputation in residence — had not only been ambushed, but was apparently being chewed half to death by a squadron of enraged Amazons, an honor guard of revolutionary (if we could only see them) vaginas.

First report arrived in a call from *Time*. Since it was his season for clichés, he could allow himself to think that of the wonders time on its spiral had wrought, none was so remarkable as the present state of his cordial relations with the Editor. There had been a period in his life when *Time* solemnly took him out in the backyard every few weeks to give him a going-over — in return he had never been able to strike back with more than a little rhetoric on *Time*'s iniquity until the mighty occasion when he captured the mistress of a Potentate of *Time*. That lady, in the final phase of an extended liaison, had most certainly been on the lookout for the particular sweet fellow who would most outrage her Boss. The Prisoner, being fresh out of Bellevue, gave money's worth. If, in a story he had once written called "The Time of Her Time," the protagonist had been fond of referring to his sexual instrument as the Avenger, now the Prizewinner whammed nothing less than a Retaliator in and out of Vengeance Mews (thereby collecting a good share of the poisons the Potentate had certainly left behind) and was so intent on retribution it took him months to recognize that the dear pudding of a lady in whom he was inserting his fast-rusting barb was a remarkable girl, almost as interesting, complex, Machiavellian, and spiritual as himself. The experience marked him profoundly (to a marriage and one of his children indeed!) he was never again so good a revolutionary — in fact, he ended as a Left Conservative.

Well, that was years ago, more than seven. He was another vessel now. Ditto America, twice transmogrified since Eisenhower days. Relations between himself and the Editor of *Time* — not to be confused with the Potentate who was long since gone — had become cordial yet wary, like logrollers from separate villages who bob and smile at one another when occupying the same log. On this day the Editor had an offer. He wished to send one of his best reporters up to Maine to do a cover story on the author's reactions to the most prominent phenomenon of the summer season:

the extraordinary surge of interest in Women's Liberation.

The air became naturally electric. It was not that either of them had simple lusts. The Editor, a sophisticated cigar if men were ever to smoke, was the first to agree equably that a cover story *could* be the kiss of death. And the Author, while courteous to the point of insisting that such a story in *Time* was bad only for the innocent and for the ambitious (when it appeared out of phase to the movements of their career) now was forced to confess that with all due respect he did not wish his face on a cover. This cost him half a true penny, for he had a film, *Maidstone*, which would soon be released — just so soon as he found a distributor who (1) liked it, (2) would pay for it, and (3) would not cheat him blind, and since the three items were to anyone who knew the film business triangularly exclusive (since a distributor who liked a film could not dream of paying for it — wasn't it enough he liked it? — and a distributor ready to give you money had calculated already how he could steal it back) there were inclinations he could detect in the sliding of his gut to have the cover story and use it in part to talk of his film (which he loved and thought superior to nearly every movie he saw). But the image of his children, those five separate beauties, all captured into cavorting

15

for *Time*'s still camera did not make him happy. One hardly knew what it might do to them. Besides, he was wifeless and his mistress was in the kitchen. She was too proper to be photographed, too proud to be passed over.

The objections half-stated, indicated, or merely hinted, the Editor came to the nut of the mission. There was no intention to make a study of the Author at home, of his family, of his private life, no, the desire was to get his opinions on Women's Lib — he was, as he knew all too well, perhaps the primary target of their attacks.

No, said the Author, he had not realized.

"Well, you may as well face it. They seem to think you're their major ideological opposition."

Now he was tempted. To be the center of any situation was, he sometimes thought, the real marrow of his bone — better to expire as a devil in the fire than an angel in the wings. His genius was to mobilize on the instant. Eight bright and razor-edged remarks leaped to his tongue at the thought of what he could say about the ladies of the Liberation, and yet the tired literary gentleman in himself curbed the studhorse of this quick impulse. Only a fool would throw serious remarks into the hopper at *Time*. The subject was too large for quick utterances: the need of the magazine reader for a remark he could repeat at the evening table was served best by writers with names like Gore Vidal; besides, it was improvident. He would be giving up substance — which is to say not making money — doing it for nothing but the possible promotion of his film, yet he knew the High Media well enough to recognize that on the moment he agreed to a cover story a process had been initiated which would eventually deposit him in a box of condensed quotations on the middle of the page of a longer story about someone else. To bite and win a cover would certainly be corrosive to any iron in the spine of his long-soaked integrity, but to bite and lose! — the dialogue ended as politely as it began.

The Prisoner of Wedlock did not brood over the conversation. For once he seemed to have made the correct decision. There was a tissue of communion between the children and himself, all too easily poked through, so it was nice that the largest woe of the weeks in Maine was the speed with which they passed. Only once in a while did he have time to remember that there was a crowd in the jail of New York with blacks and Puerto Ricans overcrowded in their cells, and ghettos simmering on the American stove, a world of junkies, hippies, freaks, and freaks who made open love at be-ins, concerts, happenings, and on the stage of tiny theaters with invited guests, plus a world of subway-goers, grim as flint and cobblestone, funky as swamps in the long armpit of dim-lit transit cars. And there were the legions of Women's Liberation. He had a vision of thin college ladies with eyeglasses, no-nonsense features, mouths thin as bologna slicers, a babe in one arm, a hatchet in the other, gray eyes bright with balefire. It was hard to think of himself as one of their leading enemies. Four times beaten at wedlock, his respect for the power of women was so large that the way they would tear through him (in his mind's eye) would be reminiscent of old newsreels of German tanks crunching through straw huts on their way across a border. He was a devout believer in the theory (which he had developed himself — *there* were his most honored beliefs!) that a chart of the social world equal in complexity to a great novel existed in better or less detail in everyone's unconscious, and therefore everyone was always bringing his chart up to date. Obviously there were some large if recent errors in his own. By the logic of survival, the Editor of *Time* had to be a man whose nose for oncoming trends was so acute that they could feed computers off his judgment. So the wave of Women's Lib, whether on the scene for a summer, a year, an era, or the duration of a great turn of the wheel of history, was then very much a phenomenon to rough in quickly on the chart, even if he had not received a clue this summer in the blue fjord of noble Somes Sound.

There had of course been intimations for the past year or more, but he had chosen to ignore them. Sitting at lunch one day in the Algonquin with the wise, responsible, and never unattractive manifestation of women's rights embodied in the political reporter of *New York* magazine, sitting at lunch when Gloria Steinem first asked him to run for mayor (and so slipped the terminal worm of political ambition into his plate) he should have had a clue, for in response to his protestations third time around that he would certainly not run, she had smiled and said, "Well, at least I won't have to explain you to my friends at Women's Lib."

"What could they have against me?"

"You might try reading your books some day."

In an interview he had once said, "Women, at their worst, are low sloppy beasts." He made reference to this now, and added, "I thought the next question would be, 'What are women at their best?' but the question never came." Enormously fond of his stratagems, he gave a Presidential smile to Gloria Steinem and added, "I would have replied that women at their best are goddesses."

"That's exactly what's wrong with your attitude."

"Exactly what's right," he answered (with a mouth full of food and oncoming polemical gusto).

But the topic was obviously too large for lunch, and besides, Miss Steinem wished him to consider the mayoralty campaign. So he did not have a chance to expatiate on the delicacies of his thought, and how every theme he had ever considered was ready to pass with profit through the question of women, their character, their destiny, their life as a class, their tyranny, their slavery, their liberation, their subjection to the wheel of nature, their root in eternity — no German metaphysician, no Doctor of Dialectics could have been happier at the thought of traveling far on the Woman Question. He was forever pleased with himself at how cleverly he had buried this as yet undisclosed vision of women in his books. (His fictional concerns after all were invariably with heroes.) No, he would yet disclose his views. But in the interim, it was his favorite indulgence to issue irritating remarks — "Women are low sloppy beasts" — or better! they would yet burn him for this — "The fact of the matter is that the prime responsibility of a woman probably is to be on earth long enough to find the best mate possible for herself, and conceive children who will improve the species." Yes, that calculated to set up interest.

Running for mayor, he ran into the redoubtable Bella

Abzug in a small meeting of ladies in a small upstairs office suite in an old building in lower Manhattan. The group — could it have been Women Strike for Peace? — was composed in good part of solemn, sensible, efficient, maternal, middle-aged, and not unsympathetic women, ladies who listened carefully and argued passionately with him. And at the center was Abzug, an embodiment so well named that the novelist could tip his hat to the great novelist in the Lord! — Bella! the future congresswoman, with bosoms which spoke of butter, milk, carnal abundance, and the firepower of hard-prowed gunboats.

"Listen," said Bella, "you came here to get our support, but we're here to look you over. We don't throw our support away for nothing. We hate phonies and we find you hard to size up." She gave him the flat look of a furniture mover unimpressed with the antique value of the heavy stuff he would soon be humping on his back. "Your record against the war in Vietnam is okay, nothing spectacular, but decent. Yet your views on women do not impress us. In fact we think they stink. We think your views on women are full of shit." She had a voice which could have boiled the fat off a taxicab driver's neck. It was as full of the vibrations of power as those machines which rout out grooves in wood. And the women listened to her intently, a few

twitching in the reflex of proper upbringing four
decades old, shuddering involuntarily at the palpable
smack of the last phrase on its way into the visiting
candidate's face. Others nodded somberly at the sound
of shit, as if to say they as women, intimates of the diapers of the mighty and the low, had more of a right to
the word than the men. And the candidate, squeezed
by schedules, irritable with brain fatigue and his own
amateurism, mired in the middle of an endless set of
days with nothing but pumped-up candidate's warmth
and the repetition of the same speech, leaped into
happy rejoinder at this broil. "Listen, Bella," he thun-
dered, his voice large for the first time in weeks, "don't
say I'm a dilettante on Vietnam. I was telling them to
hang LBJ's photo upside down when all of you were
still singing 'Hello, Lyndon.'" Shameless. He was quoting himself from *The Armies of the Night*. But that was
the trouble with politics. It rendered every pride.

"Where do you get away with this?" asked Abzug.

"Furthermore," — it was the first time he had ever
used so curdled a banquet word, but he saw its political
function now, *furthermore* was full of narrative promise, and so helped you to hold a yaw in the floor —
"*Feu de mort*, I can tell you that regardless of my views
on women, as *you* think you know them, women in any
administration I could run would have more voice,

22

more respect, more real opportunity for real argument than any of the other candidates would offer you. What is our campaign promise of Power to the Neighborhoods but an offering to Women's Liberation? Do you think Herman Badillo" (a reference to his nearest ideological opponent) "respects you more because he'll come in and kiss your collective ass? You know perfectly well I'm the only one who's ready to talk straight to the people of New York regardless of their political ideas or mine and confess my mistakes, and save this city by the only way it can be saved — by giving the power back to the people who live in this city. Which of the other candidates is ready to tell you ladies that?"

It was the best short speech he had gotten off in days. His greatest deficiency in politics was that he could not usually sell himself. Yes, a good speech, that he could tell by the softening of Bella Abzug's regard, and indeed there was nothing so promising, so warm, so indicative of a hearty future in politics as the melting of a battle-ax. He was enormously fond of Bella at this instant. For it was her stentorian force, her bullying wall-slamming style of address which had awakened him, given him strength for the moment. So it was the part of the meeting he remembered, rather than the more careful and intelligent colloquy which followed on the merits of a women's march to Washington. And he ignored entirely the reference to his views on women which in fact did not come up again except for his tacit recognition that the discussion had been concerted and intelligent, nay more to the point than some of the oratorical gymkhana at his own staff meetings.

Passing intimations — that was all. Months later, perhaps a half year later, a book arrived, one of the half-dozen that week. (He was forever receiving books or bound sets of galleys with the cool or fervent hopes of the editor enclosed — sometimes he thought it would be easier for young authors to make a fortune by playing the numbers than waiting for an established author to bless a book which came unsolicited in the mail.)

This book, however, had a letter attached which informed him that *Thinking About Women,* by Mary Ellmann, had more references to his own name in the index than any other writer — could he comment? Pleased at this evidence that the wave was once again on the way, and he was the name of that wave, he discovered instead that the references were pinpricks, bitchy pinpricks, caustic pinpricks, aloof — one hardly felt the point — and disdainful pinpricks, on occasion pricks which were downright unfair. Forty such pricks. He did not read them all — after ten, he gave up the thought of finding mercy in Mrs. Ellmann's club.

The book was dismissed. Nonetheless, *Thinking About Women* intrigued him now and again, for it was well written, even if its analysis of his work was reminiscent of the calisthenics an FBI agent might assign a Weatherman. "Keep those push-ups coming" was not unequal to ". . . always thrashing quality. At his best, he has a desperate bravado, a last-standness which becomes a way of extracting some vitality, like clotting blood, from defunct opinions. . . . It will not be admitted, by Mailer, that even the bowels move without personal meaning, the sewers reek with messages. . . . One is reminded of the fundamental grimness with which Norman Mailer thinks of every pickle or ice-cream cone as an index of intestinal morality" — yes, that was fair, for it suggested a colloquy between the liver's passions and the justified claims of the spleen, the spirituality of the lungs in conflict with the wage demands of the muscles, all subjected at last to the logic of intestinal morality where the funerals were planned, yes, sharp criticism always kissed your thought up another notch. His strength was to love the job a good critic could do on him — in this regard, he was equal to one of those prodigies of paradoxical health who thrive on operation after operation — his literary vitality seemed to derive from being exposed. But a critic who took unfair advantage (when there was all that real meat to slice!)

was like a surgeon who mashed his thumb on the edge of the incision before sewing it up. Now, sad to witness, the lady — like many a male critic before her — was beginning to tip the scales. She could not speak with balance about *An American Dream.* "His imagination is offended by a combined odor of clam shells, salt marshes, female bodies and sickening brews — 'perfumes which leave the turpentine of a witch's curse.' Choking with sexual disgust (fresh sheets! fresh air!) he describes a nose's nightmare. The witch herself is dead, Mailer smells her unwashed corpse."

But this was no longer a metaphorical FBI agent treating him like a Weatherman — this was a lady kicking him in the nuts. All that sexual disgust attributed to him, all that imputation that he was crying for fresh sheets, all suggestion that it was his association of clam shells and female bodies, were actually a set of connections which existed only in her mind. *Her* mind was on the clam. Yes, for her witch's unwashed corpse to be arbitrarily thrown in with his witch's turpentine curse was straight abuse of the critic's function. Ellmann's nostrils were too hairy with the heat to kill. So he closed the book without embarking on it, closed her book with the firm prejudice that if she could not be fair to him, she could not be fair to her theme; yet closed it with sour regret, since the lady wrote well.

Somewhere in this time, he glanced at an article by Kate Millett in *New American Review*. He read only a few lines, but it was enough to think she wrote like a gossip columnist. *"An American Dream* is an exercise in how to kill your wife and be happy ever after." He forgot Millett, even forgot Ellmann, forgot them to so nice a point in the labors of trying to create a modicum of style about technology and the moon that he was not certain which of the two ladies was being discussed when first he heard talk of a book, indeed of a bible of liberation which newspaper reviews intimated would succeed at last — hoarse was the phlegm of the snicker — in separating the female from her womb. The book was *Sexual Politics* and the author proved to be the second of the ladies he had not bothered to read. Six weeks after his conversation with the Editor of *Time,* Kate Millett's face was on the cover.

He did not know why a lack of such literary niceties as fair quotation and measured attack should bother him more in women. Was it because a male critic who practiced such habits could not go far — the stern code of professionalism in other men was bound to cut him down; or was it because unfairness in women rubbed that larger question (with its affiliate wounds and guilts) of what he had done to women over the years and what women had done to him. That could open the melancholy of his life, for he was never so near to the Old Testament as with the primitive belief that one's children were the blessing or the curse, and his children were on most days scattered.

Nonetheless, he was obliged to be aware that he provoked the issue endlessly — better to be the devil in the fire! Just a week before he left for the summer in Maine he had actually found himself saying one night on a television program (in reply to a question from Orson Welles) that women should be kept in cages.

He had grinned broadly as he said this, delighted with the gasp which came up from the audience. Television audiences always reminded him of the bathers at Acapulco. The temperature of the air was ninety degrees, the temperature of the water was ninety degrees — one passed from one medium to the other with a minimum of sensation. So, too, was the passage of comment on television. Therefore this last bright sentiment poured ice cubes down everyone's back. He could feel electrons shuddering. And was pleased with himself, pleased that he might be the last of the public entertainers to cut such an outsized hunk of remark in the teeth of growing piety over the treatment of women. Even Welles was solemn about the matter.

Later in the program, he said, "Well now, since you admit you hate women . . ."

"But I don't hate women."

"You said you did."

"No, I said they should be kept in cages." The trouble with television is that you had to give direct responses, and most of his ideas were paradoxes — he could say, "We will be able to reduce the birthrate only when we stop practicing contraception," but it would take a long piece of writing to explain why he thought this. So the impulse to clown was inevitable. But then he had to rush to take the edge off the remark before he was branded with it. "Orson, we respect the lions in the zoo, but we want them kept in cages, don't we?"

What romantic zeal to think an audience would seize the dialectical spring of the idea, would recognize that no man who thought women should be kept in cages would ever dare to declare such a sentiment. Think of the retribution! No, the machines were moving in to replace such humor. The flat reaction of the television audience reminded him of his most pessimistic belief — that the spirit of the twentieth century was to convert man to a machine. If that were so, then the liberation of women might be a trap. So, when he came back from Maine it was with, yes, the gloomy and growing sense that he would have to write about women, about their

liberation and the drear pits in the road of that liberation, and the PW was gloomy twice, for there would
be something ludicrous in the effort, ludicrous that a
man who bobbed in waves of controversy like a cork
with a comic dent should elect himself as spokesman
for the topic. Who was he to know more of women than
any stud or ski bum who did not care to speak? Or any
good and faithful husband who was too weary to
speak? But then it was ludicrous twice, since he could
not even enter the question without defending himself.
A defendant could serve as his own lawyer, but not as
his own judge. By his presence in the discussion he
would be forced to occupy all the seats.

Yet the themes of his life had gathered here. Revolution, tradition, sex and the homosexual, the orgasm, the
family, the child and the political shape of the future,
technology and human conception, waste and abortion,
the ethics of the critic and the male mystique, black
rights and new thoughts on women's rights — the
themes were pervasive enough to depress him. For the
themes also belonged to that huge novel he had promised to begin so many times. To trick some of these
ideas forth now was to play danger with his book — at
the least to write about Women's Liberation with
honest force would be equal to playing the Saturday
night music on Tuesday night, and that most unhappily

was what he was into now. That was what he was into now. Let others beware of receiving the reputation that it is women they do not like. For the PW was now off on a search and knew that the longer he looked, the less we would see of him. On came the ladies with their fierce ideas.

II The Acolyte

THE DEPTH OF THE JOB did not delight him. How much easier, he could not help but think, to have gone forth, notebook in hand, to give a running account of further adventures of the Prisoner of

Wedlock on a journalistic beat. But his instinct was not to approach the subject this way. To embark on a round of interviews with the leading ladies of Women's Liberation was likely to produce a piece not unreminiscent of an article in the *New Yorker*. You had to hang the subject of the interview when the subject was in the position of selling his ideas. It was always necessary to remind oneself that a series of such interviews with Lenin, Martov, Plekhanov, and Trotsky in the days of *Iskra* would have been likely to produce a set of stories about short stocky men in rumpled clothes and unhealthy beards who seemed to talk with a great deal of certainty in words which were hard to follow. Obviously, no journalist could have done the job — it was work which called for a novelist, or a critical approach, and the last was certain to return the burden to the reader. Still he had no choice. The only decent way to approach the liberation of women was by the writing of participants. Recognize his surprise when some of the writing was agreeable.

No matter that the voices were almost familiar and the ring of more than a few pieces remained close to the ladies' magazines, while piety occasionally declared, "Now, I possess the truth, poor formerly misguided me!" women still emerged with an authority he had not encountered in such casual writing before. If there was small echo of the Bolsheviks, they were none-theless not without the force of many voices. Whether angry or introspective, the voices were a hint disturbing; some trace of a Martian was in the air, or was it the experience of a complex animal finally revealed? — he was obviously no more accustomed than anyone else to females offering direct speech.

A young woman is walking down a city street. She is excruciatingly aware of her appearance and of the reaction to it (imagined or real) of every person she meets. She walks through a group of construction workers who are eating lunch in a line along the pavement. Her stomach tightens with terror and revulsion; her face becomes contorted into a grimace of self-control and fake unawareness; her walk and carriage become stiff and dehumanized. No matter what they say to her, it will be unbearable. She knows that they will not physically assault her or hurt her. They will only do so metaphorically. What they will do is impinge *on her. They will demand that her thoughts be focussed on them. They will use her body with their eyes. They will evaluate her market price. They will comment on her defects, or compare them to those of other passersby. They will make her a participant in their fantasies without asking if she is willing. They will make her feel ridiculous, or grotesquely sexual, or hideously ugly. Above all, they will make her feel like a* thing.[1]

It was the natural condition of a woman in such a situation, he was obliged to recognize, and yet any man

feeling so stripped of his skin would be suffering an unholy mix of narcissism and paranoia. Inner conditions
like that were usually reserved for combat, for committing a robbery (when even the furniture looks at
you) or on the first day in jail. From the point of view
of the man, it was as if women were obliged to live on
that existential edge in which the application of make-
up has an echo of the forest.

The incredible elation of looking in a mirror (the lighting
just right . . .) and seeing, not the familiar plain, trouble-
some self, but a beautiful object, not ourself, but a thing
outside, a beautiful thing, worthy of worship . . . no one
could resist falling in love with such a face.[2]

If there is an impact in such candor, "If we are going
to be liberated we must reject the false image that
makes men love us, and this will make men cease to
love us," [3] the women just quoted are still speaking as
women obsessed with their relation to men. Others
proceeded to shift the focus to themselves.

. . . I no longer need a man. Until recently, even as I ac-
tively struggled for my liberation, it was with a part of me
still reserved for "men only." I always thought I would end
up living with one man. I suppose that is still a possibility,
but now it is only one of many. Instead of that, I think
about living with women because the emotional and psy-

chological interchange is so satisfying. I have begun to reclaim my body; discovering what it can do, how strong it can be, and how thought is not something that takes place in the mind alone. I no longer see myself through men's eyes, as capable of certain things only, but with my own eyes, as a healthy person with a lot of endurance and determination that I haven't used before. There are signs that I may yet discover what I like to do, which is very different from trying to figure out what men and society in general expect of me.[4]

If he had also to read his way through dull and piteous tracts, whining and catarrhal styles, ponderous intestinal coils of prose reminiscent of the worst of the old party line, if, when all was counted, the books directly on the theme were few and the articles dispersed in twenty hopeful magazines and forty underground sheets, still, the shock continued, and other pieces brought him short. Impossible to avoid the conclusion. A few of the women were writing in no way women had ever written before. If, among young male writers, a style had begun to evolve over the past ten years which owed something to the tone of the *Village Voice*, the *East Village Other,* and a dozen underground papers he had seen from coast to coast, if the language of the blacks was in that style and the language of prison and junk and the writings on the

39

walls of public bathrooms, now the women were using it. Some of the women were writing like very tough faggots. It was a good style. At its best, it read with the tension of an anger profound enough to be kept under the skin. Every point was made with a minimum of words, a mean style, no question of that. It used obscenity with the same comfort a whore would take with her towel.

A Bitch occupies a lot of psychological space. You always know she is around. A Bitch takes shit from no one. You may not like her, but you cannot ignore her.[5]

The sex life of spiders is very interesting. He fucks her. She bites off his head.[6]

. . . When you get into listening to male rock lyrics, the message to women is devastating. We are cunts, sometimes ridiculous (Twentieth Century Fox), sometimes mysterious (Ruby Tuesday), sometimes bitchy (Get a Job) and sometimes just plain cunts (Wild Thing). And all that sexual energy that seems to be the essence of rock is really energy that climaxes in fucking over women — endless lyrics and a sound filled with feelings I thought I was relating to but couldn't relate to — attitudes about women like putdowns, domination, threats, pride, mockery, fucking around and a million different levels of woman hating.[7]

The Prisoner was sufficiently cynical about underground papers to believe a man could have written such prose to smuggle across his idea of how a female should speak, but the editorial office of *Rat* (where the last piece appeared) had been seized in a coup d'etat by shock troops from Women's Liberation. It was doubtful such militant ladies would accept writing which came through the transom. Besides, there were always more examples to offer.

CROTCH CLAWERS
And Mother Rapers of the World:
come out of your stinking womb
that is no part of the woman who gave you birth.
Realize a few things about me.
(I am sick of playing your *game)*

You say that i, a woman,
should be more sensitive
to the ways which you oppress me

At the same time, i, a woman
am by nature a bitch.
Well your coldness
it turns me bitchier by the hour.

Self-fulfilling prophecy:
Woman are evil, sneeky and wicked.
Shit.
You are the one who asked for it.

> *Tomorrow a couple of Father Fuckers*
> *may be on* your *ass.*

— *pati trolander*

(*I have only been alive 14 years, how am I*
going to feel 10 years from now?)[8]

Already the style had crossed the Atlantic. Published
in Upper James Street, Golden Square, London, *The*
Female Eunuch by Germaine Greer, a work to "inspire
and incite any woman with any pride, imagination and
sense of moral responsibility," [9] had been able to produce the next quotations.

The worst name anyone can be called is cunt. *The best*
thing a cunt can be is small and unobtrusive: the anxiety
about the bigness of the penis is only equalled by anxiety
about the smallness of the cunt. No woman wants to find
out that she has a twat like a horse-collar: she hopes she
is not sloppy or smelly, and obligingly obliterates all signs
of her menstruation in the cause of public decency.

Women still buy sanitary towels with enormous discre-
tion, and carry their handbags to the loo when they only
need to carry a napkin. They still recoil at the idea of inter-
course during menstruation, and feel that the blood they
shed is of a special kind, although perhaps not so special
as was thought when it was the liquid presented to the
devil in witches' loving cups. If you think you are emanci-

pated, you might consider the idea of tasting your men-
strual blood — if it makes you sick, you've a long way to
go, baby.[10]

A wind in this prose whistled up the kilts of male
conceit. The base of male conceit was that men could
live with truths too unsentimental for women to support (hence the male mind was gifted with superior
muscles just so much as the back) now women were
writing about men and about themselves as Henry
Miller had once written about women, which is to say,
with all the gusto of a veterinarian getting into the
glisten of the chancre in a show mare's dock. What a
shock! The Prizewinner recognized all over again that
he had much to learn on many a familiar topic.

2

There was an idea at the core of Women's
Liberation which was fundamentally radical and so could not be ignored unless
he were willing to cease thinking of himself as a revolutionary. Well, he was willing in all the well-oiled pockets of all his middle-aged
pleasures, but the country wasn't. Damn smog! Damn

filthy polluted anomalous greed-choked monster-breeding machine of an inchoate land — it forced one daily back to the all but used-up revolutionary of the spirit.

So the revolution called again, close to farce, that ill-mannered, drug-leached, informer-infested, indiscriminate ripping up of all the roots, yes, spoiled young middle-class heroes with fleas in their beard and rashes doubtless in the groin were accelerating each other now to accelerate America into the straightest fascism of them all. And agents provocateurs in every cell. Yet he could not condemn them. Society, left to itself, blissfully void of revolutionaries, would expire in a welter of the most liberal sentiments and the foulest air, die in the total ecological disruption of the universe, if indeed the insane economic imbalances of the cities did not burst forth first. In the center of such cauldrons, who could know if the inability of men to administer a world which would not destroy itself was ultimately the fault of all those women who had exhausted the best of their men, or if the blame belonged to the men? Still, his sympathies remained with his own sex. If he had begun this remedial reading with the firmest male prejudice of them all, which is that women might possess the better half of life already, he was never to encounter any comprehension among female writers that a firm erection on a delicate fellow was the adven-

turous juncture of ego and courage. One attitude in
Women's Lib remained therefore repellent: precisely
the dull assumption that the sexual force of a man was
the luck of his birth, rather than his finest moral product, or if not his — here, full blast, came genuine conservatism — then a local gift passed along by something well achieved in his mother, his father, or farther
back the line.

Yes, men were relatively fragile. Never to doubt it.
He had seen too many women down too many men,
some with a campaign of applied force masterful as
Grant on the way to Appomattox, some by the simple
frustration of what was best in her mate at the best of
times — not for nothing had he long considered the
first of Hemingway stories to be "The Short Happy Life
of Francis Macomber." Before the depth of subtlety in
an attractive and dishonest woman, how much more
chance for an honest lover than a brave bull? And before the depth of rage in an unattractive woman, a man
could look for home life on the assembly line.

Of course, the claim could hardly be entered that
men were helpless before women. It was a near-equal
war after all, a brutal bloody war with wounds growing
within and the surgeons collecting the profit from
either sex. But finally, by his measure of these matters,
he had seen too many men who failed to accomplish

what they desired because a woman had ground them down, and had seen even more women who never discovered what they desired, and on the consequence set out to hobble their men. "The great question that has never been answered, and which I have not yet been able to answer despite my thirty years of research into the feminine soul, is: What does a woman want?" Not for nothing had Freud been the author of the remark; not for nothing were women in the Liberation forever quoting it since now they believed they were ready to offer their reply. Out of the silence of the centuries came the reply. It was: the reality of the rib is equal to the reality of Adam. If the penis, at rest, might be 10 cubic inches, whereas an average man or woman was probably 3,000 cubic inches, ergo, men and women were 99⅔ percent identical, or as 299 parts in 300. What! — who cannot hear the argument! — what of the womb and the testicles? the breasts and . . . But of course the argument did not yet exist — it was only a tendency. Listen:

Life in this society being, at best, an utter bore and no aspect of society being at all relevant to women, there remains to civic-minded, responsible, thrill-seeking females only to overthrow the government, eliminate the money system, institute complete automation, and destroy the male sex.

It is now technically possible to reproduce without the aid of males (or, for that matter, females) and to produce only females. We must begin immediately to do so. The male is a biological accident: the Y (male) gene is an incomplete X (female) gene, that is, has an incomplete set of chromosomes. In other words, the male is an incomplete female, a walking abortion, aborted at the gene state.[11]

The words are from SCUM, the Society for Cutting Up Men. The author, who comprised the total membership of SCUM, is Valerie Solanis, who fired a gun into Andy Warhol and almost succeeded in killing him. It is to the honor of the editors of an anthology on Women's Liberation, *Sisterhood Is Powerful* (a title of obvious totalitarian propensities) that the SCUM Manifesto is included, since it is hardly difficult for enemies of the sisters to score points at this place. Yet the SCUM Manifesto, while extreme, even extreme of the extreme, is nonetheless a magnetic north for Women's Lib. All their lines of intellectual magnetism flow away from Adam's rib — male manifesto to suggest that woman is no more than a phallus come to life — and converge on Valerie Solanis and her Manifesto. Even the word, scum, will give a quiver to any woman with memories of a mouthful of unwanted semen in her throat. "Being an incomplete female," the Manifesto goes on, *the male spends his life attempting to complete himself, to become female. He attempts to do this by constantly seeking out, fraternizing with and trying to live through and fuse with the female, and by claiming as his own all female characteristics — emotional strength and independence, forcefulness, dynamism, decisiveness, coolness, objectivity, assertiveness, courage, integrity, vitality, intensity, depth of character, grooviness, etc. — and projecting onto women all male traits — vanity, frivolity, triviality, weakness, etc. It should be said, though, that the male has one glaring area of superiority over the female — public relations. (He has done a brilliant job of convincing millions of women that men are women and women are men.) The male claim that females find fulfillment through motherhood and sexuality reflects what males think they'd find fulfilling if they were females.*

Women, in other words, don't have penis envy; men have pussy envy . . .

Pussy envy! Three quarters of the men in the world, bewildered by complexities for which there was no solution, no precedent, no leader, and no guide, must by now be ready to lay down the dread weight of a man and pick up the onerous burden of the woman. Pussy envy. Yes, three quarters of the men in the world might have it by now, have it just as secretly as the ruling classes of the nineteenth century must have wished for the simple life of the farmer, the worker, and the shopgirl; yes, the argument that women were a social and economic class exploited by a ruling class of men, that women were finally the largest and most exploited class of them all, more exploited than workers, colonial peoples, and blacks (since women were everywhere exploited and when black, laboring class, or colonial, twice exploited), was an argument which could at last begin to exist in the everyday of common consciousness.

Yet, studying the reply he was obliged to recognize that no matter how prejudiced he might be in favor of the men, the life of the argument was still on the side of the women: for if women were the true aggressors in this primal war, what indeed could be done? If smog, civil war, foreign war, drugs, and the male's loss of confidence that he could properly run the world were insidious female accomplishments — then female success was Satanic, and the world was lost. Once decide, however, that the men were to blame, and there was hope: a revolution of women could open every social disease to the beneficent examination of a new human light. No choice then but to remind himself that he had not set out to collect the most entertaining exhibits of a new intellectual fashion but rather to explore the revolutionary ideas which emerged from these collective pamphlets, books, and bible of Women's Lib, and explore them with all awareness that they were twentieth-century ideas, and so might be

49

artfully designed to advance the fortunes of the on-coming technology of the state. What a paranoid supposition was this! Yet how reasonable. Paranoia and common sense come together as the world goes insane.

3

Women were indeed a class if one saw them in terms of their economic treatment. There the statistics were clear and overwhelming. One could of course make a formal study of the subject. The PW was sufficiently intimate with magazine readers to know the age of technology had left them with an inability to respect writing which lacked the authority of statistics (even if they passed over the numbers and rushed to the dialogue). So he was used to paying the formal respect of offering a few digits and wheeling in a few legislative proposals, and would do it here again, and soon! — but always he performed this expository chore with the resentment that it was only a convention and so would encourage the mind of the reader to desert him for a period (which was about as agreeable to a writer as it is agreeable to a lover to recognize that at just this point in the act, the sweet female mind between his hands has begun to think of nothing less than the laundry list).

Nonetheless! In 1964, income for a working female was $3,710; for the male, $6,233. Therefore the median wages of women were barely 60 percent of the wages of men. Of the Americans who earned more than $10,000 a year, only 2 percent were women. In the professions, 7 percent of the doctors were women, 3 percent of the lawyers, and 1 percent of the engineers. In America — where one did not expect such differences — even men opposed to Women's Liberation were willing to agree that the economic exploitation of the female was a condition in need of amendment.

Armed with Valerie Solanis, we know the argument pushes beyond that point — indeed the Prizewinner, first encountering the economic argument, could tell by his readiness to offer tribute that he was covertly hoping women would thereby be satisfied, and knew, by the depression which followed, they wouldn't. The women were also looking for a cultural revolution and a sexual revolution. The real argument was that they could not obtain economic equality without either of the others. Of course, most women (in common with the male political animal) hesitated to look for the real argument, so he was obliged to mention that just as more Negroes had been active in NAACP or the Urban League than had joined SNCC or the Black Panthers, so female groups divided in similar proportion: more belonged in sympathy to the moderate demands of women's rights than the radical demands of Liberation. (Of course we know whether we would rather read about the Urban League or the Black Panthers.) Still —he could not escape his informational responsibilities — the largest group in the women's movement was founded by Betty Friedan, author of *The Feminine Mystique,* had nothing less than five thousand members, was called NOW (National Organization for Women) and looked to achieve its demands through lobbying and legislation. Its Bill of Rights, adopted at a national conference in Washington, D.C., had eight liberal rallying points, eight legislative points of pressure guaranteed to separate the left wing of the Democratic party from the right (and the collective mind of his readers from his prose), for these eight points, even abbreviated, called for a Constitutional Amendment giving equal rights under the law to women, a law banning sex discrimination in employment, "immediate revision of tax laws to permit the deduction of home and child-care expenses for working parents," "child-care facilities established by law on the same basis as

parks, libraries, and public schools," "the right of
women to be educated to their full potential equally
with men . . . at all levels of education," revision of
welfare laws to provide women with more "dignity,
privacy, and self-respect," the right of women to go
back to their jobs "after childbirth without loss of sen-
iority . . . and be paid maternity leave as a form of
social security." Finally, "the right of women to control
their own reproductive lives by . . . access to contraceptive information and devices, and by repealing
penal laws governing abortion." [12]

Eight firm points, and given the fibrous legislative
growths in many a state constitution, and pussy envy
being what it was, years would go by before the last
of those reasonable demands would become a legal
commonplace, but woe to the liberal politician who
was not quickly conversant with them; yes, so far as
the federal government could take just care of the
needs of the people, so the federal government would
have to take more and more *intimate* care of these
needs — the old war between the Old Guard and the
New Deal would thereby find new issues every decade, every year: the Bill of Rights of the National
Organization for Women would have the happy facil-
ity to be the center of these new issues. So a perspective opens of exposés of corruption in child-care cen-

ters, of Ultra Mafia Modern in new co-ed dormitories, of maternity leave and income tax revision for the working parent, balanced by oil tax reduction for pollution-free gasolines.

But his cynic's blood was reinforced by the iron of a radical pamphlet, a modest article on mimeographed sheets with a yellow cover, modest even to the price, thirty cents, and the address, an unassuming address, 3800 McGee, Kansas City. The author was Linda Phelps, a name he had not particularly encountered before, and her article was nothing famous, but reminiscent of the best of old socialist and trade-union writers and so was a way of reminding him again that women everywhere were certainly learning how to write on many a male subject. Bearing the somewhat Leninist title "What Is the Difference?" the piece gave him nostalgia for a nonexistent time in which he had thought in just such a forthright fashion. Of course, the article was also to the point on the difference between liberal and radical feminism:

In contrast to NOW's concrete list of legislative proposals, Women's Liberation appears vague because we talk about solutions which aren't apparent to most women, solutions which don't exist at all in anything we can point to in the U.S. like new families, the liberation of children, the end of traditional notions of masculinity and feminin-

ity. Yet this problem should not be surprising when we consider that it has kept women in their place for so long.

We have made two basic contentions about a program of women's rights — that women will not respond to an appeal to live the kind of lives they see men living and that if they tried to do so in large numbers, they would cause a crisis in society. The two reasons are interconnected. . . . The women's rights movement will never get anywhere, it seems to me, as long as it sees the problem as equal participation in American life, because women will never risk whatever positions of security they do have and move for anything less than NEW LIVES.

The system must be seen as a whole. . . . Since 1945 we have spent one trillion dollars on military expenditures and $25 billion of that on weapons which were obsolete as soon as they were produced. Our priorities are not day-care centers and hospitals; our priority is preserving our empire, as we have demonstrated by our activities in Viet Nam. It is useless to think that women are going to get what they want and be able to live as full human beings without facing and changing this vast system of waste and exploitation which is our present economic system.[13]

Linda Phelps was probably right, he concluded with gloom; once again, women (and men as well) would not get anything fundamental without changing the economic system. And yet . . . Beyond Linda Phelps was Valerie Solanis, even as Robespierre was beyond Rousseau. A murderous inflammation of the will was inevitably waiting if power came and the revolutionary

was not its equal, just as the devil was obliged to enlarge from a spore to a fever if a clerk put on the majes-
ties of a king. Purple metaphor, but he was not a prisoner for nothing. Somewhere at the end of the line was
the enigma of revolution. If there had been a period
when he believed completely in the tonic overhauling
of the state and had written his prose with fingers trem-
bling with anger at the Establishment, he had by now
lost that essential belief in himself which was critical
to the idea that one could improve the world (and
knew he might not regain that belief until he had written the novel of his life and succeeded in passing judgment on himself — if indeed one could) no, now there
were days when he wondered if that continuing revolution of reason which the Renaissance had begun was
not a war to liberate man, but to pollute him by the
wastes of his vanity, huge scientific vanity now de-
stroying every natural act of nature. Right on! Wom-
en's Liberation, if it accomplished nothing else, had
pushed him back into an obsession he wished to quit
— which was whether the revolution was the most
beautiful or diabolical idea of man — a hateful question: because thoughts about the revolution were never
too far from thoughts about the size of his waist and
the potential humphreys of his ass. Yet he was per-
versely happier with Solanis than with Phelps, happier

because Solanis enabled one to laugh at men and women handicapping the final line on one another. Whereas Phelps, with her modest prose, was drilling holes in concrete — "What if she's right?" was again his gloomy thought.

Still, no quiet answer was going to give him rest. Beyond the economic revolution and the cultural revolution was the sexual revolution the author did not mention; perhaps there was in her style a hint of that modest aversion to the discussion of sex which delineates the good socialist. Yes, beyond Phelps was still the sexual revolution and there was a true work in coming to terms with that. For a forecast of the terms, who better to call upon than Kate Millett?

A sexual revolution would require, perhaps first of all, an end of traditional sexual inhibitions and taboos, particularly those that most threaten patriarchal monogamous marriage: homosexuality, "illegitimacy," adolescent, pre- and extra-marital sexuality. The negative aura with which sexual activity has generally been surrounded would necessarily be eliminated, together with the double standard and prostitution. The goal of revolution would be a permissive single standard of sexual freedom, and one uncorrupted by the crass and exploitative economic bases of traditional sexual alliances.[14]

The style is suggestive of a night-school lawyer who sips Metrecal to keep his figure, and thereby is so full of isolated proteins, factory vitamins, reconstituted cyclamates, and artificial flavors that one has to pore over the passages like a business contract. What explosives are buried in those droning clauses, those chains of familiar aggregates (of words).

4

In all previous consideration of class warfare there had been at least the assumption that the design of human beings was adequate, unbiased, functional, and not particularly in need of alteration. It was assumed that if the working class took over the functions of the ruling class, they would still be able to act with the conventional organs of men. But the ultimate logic of the sexual revolution required women to stand equal to the male body in every aspect — how could this equality prevail if women in competition with the other sex for the role of artist, executive, bureaucrat, surgeon, auto mechanic, politician, or masterful lover should have to cry quits every now and again for months of pregnancy plus years of uneasy accommodation between their career and their child, or else choose to have no children and so be obsessed with the possibility of biological harm, worse, the possibility of some unnameable harm to that inner space of creation their bodies would enclose?

One could speak of men and women as the poles of the universe, the universal Yang and Yin, offer views of the Creation in such abstract lands as seed and womb, vision and firmament, fire up a skyworks of sermon and poem to the incontestable mystery that women are flesh of the Mystery more than men — it would not diminish by a coulomb those electrics of wrath in the eyes of those women whose revolutionary principles are Jacobin. It was as if the High Grand *Geist* of the Jacobins had returned to state, "It was never enough to sever the heads of the aristocrats. The time is now come to get the first Aristocrat of them all. Since He designed women at a disadvantage, such Work must be overthrown!"

What a job! Men were by comparison to women as simple meat; men were merely human beings equipped to travel through space at a variety of speeds, but women were human beings traveling through the same variety of space in full possession of a mysterious space within. In that purse of flesh were psychic tendrils, waves of communication to some conceivable source of life, some manifest of life come into human beings from a beyond which persisted in remaining most

59

stubbornly beyond. Women, like men, were human beings, but they were a step, or a stage, or a move or a leap nearer the creation of existence, they were — given man's powerful sense of the present — his indispensable and only connection to the future; how could a woman compete if she contained the future as well as the present and so lived a physical life on the edge of the divide? What punishment traveled into the future with the pile driver's clang? whose unborn ear heard the loss of a note in the squawk of the static? The womb was a damnable disadvantage in the struggle with the men, a cranky fouled-up bag of horrors for any woman who would stand equal to man on modern jobs, for technology was the domain of number, of machines and electronic circuits, of plastic surfaces, static, vibrations, and contemporary noise. Yet through all such disturbance, technology was still built on conformity of practice. If it could adjust to rhythm, tide, the ebb of mood, and the phasing in and phasing out of energy in the men and women who worked its machines, nonetheless such adjustments were dear to technology, for each departure from a uniform beat demanded a new expensive control. The best operator was the uniform operator, and women had that unmentionable womb, that spongy pool, that time machine with a curse, dam for an ongoing river of blood whose rhythm seemed to obey some private compact with the moon. How this womb, unaccountable liaison with the beyond, disrupted every attempt at uniform behavior!

Did women get into automobile accidents? Count on it, more than half their accidents came on a particular week of the month — just before and during menstruation was the time of that week. So, too, were almost half of the female admissions to mental hospitals in that week, and more than half of their attempted suicides, half the crimes committed by women prisoners. "Yet her knowledge of the womb is academic: most women do not actually feel any of the activity of their ovaries or womb until they go wrong, *as they nearly always do.* Many women, one might say too many women die of illnesses in organs that they have virtually ignored all their lives, the cervix, the vulvae, the vagina and the womb." [15] (A man trying to take cognizance of this might have to picture an existence where carcinoma of the cock and balls was close to the common fate.) Yes, afloat in some river of time she did not see (womblike was the metaphor of Thomas Wolfe!), victim of "unpleasantness, odour, stainings which takes up anything from a seventh to a fifth of her adult life until the menopause . . . fertile thirteen times a year when she only expects to bear twice in a lifetime . . ." [16] yes, a victim of a relationship to certain murmurings of eternity, it is not so unnatural to react with rage against a mystical communion which condemns her to diapers, dishes, and the foul shock of unforgiving cramps, not to mention an unbroken string of defeats in her attempt to take over control of the world from men. No, the defeat was built in.

> . . . *She was never free. Her relative physical weakness and her dependence on the man during her continual pregnancies gave him an advantage he only consolidated and never relinquished.*[17]

It was here that feminism had always come to a halt, and all discussion of women as a class would terminate before the mysterious advantage and burden of her womb. Now she ceased to be a class and became a privileged element of nature, closer to the mysteries than men.

It was nonetheless intolerable. So deeply had woman entered into the spirit of the age — into the clang of the pile driver and the squall of the static — that no intellectual gift became so dear as the right to think of herself as an exploited class. For that power she was ready to turn the purse inside out. "Such Work must be overthrown!" Discussions of radical women passed even beyond the sexual revolution with its insistence on a "single standard of sexual freedom" all permissive, all hierarchies of moral precedence bombarded, all eschatologies withdrawn. Yes, the argument went beyond that quite foreseeable time when monogamy and legitimacy would be gone, when distinctions between heterosexuality would be gone, adolescent sexuality and extramarital sexuality all gone — all part of that huge revolutionary statement that all fucking high or low, by any hole or any pit, was pleasure, and pleasure was the first sweetmeat of reason. Whatever stood in the way of reason was foul.

Well, conception stood in the way of reason, for conception was embarkation on a train whose stations were obligation and guilt. That was no pleasure, no more than the bleedings of the womb. So, contraception became woman's most intimate introduction to the abilities of technology to solve delicate problems. What an unpleasantness to discover the abilities were limited — "that one woman in three . . . on the pill was chronically depressed." [18] Still, faith in technology hardly weakened. It was merely a question of replacing middling techniques with superior techniques. A spin-off, for example, in hydraulics offered hope for quick abortion.

A tubular curette, with a hole in the side of its tip, is introduced into the uterus. The curette is attached to a tube,

*a vacuum pump, and a receptacle; a slight negative air
pressure loosens the fetus, which is sucked through the
hole and passes down the tube into the receptacle. The
entire process takes about two minutes . . .*[19]

TECHNOLOGY SUCKS would appear on no placards carried by the women. The Work of the Aristocrat had
first to be demolished. His vaults, His buttresses, His
heavenly arch, yes, cess and riddance to the days of
honest abortion when the fingernails of the surgeon
were filthy and the heart of a woman went screaming
through a cave as steel scraped at the place where she
touched the beyond. "Shit, no," said the ladies. "Suck
the fucker out."

For dreams of horror and guilt were not what women
needed, far from it — they searched for a technique
which would create a proper instrument for them, a
cutting tool for an exploited class. Tentative sugges-
tions arose. From a lady named Dana Densmore, from
a journal called *No More Fun and Games:*

*In lower animals it is common for the creation of the
new cell and the early stages of its growth to take place
within the body of the female, where it takes nourishment
from the body of the female. The female human being is
also equipped to do this. However, there is no more reason
for her to continue to bear this burden suggested by the
anatomy.*

Man freed himself from this burden, this inconvenience,

this inadaptability by fashioning clothes. Similarly, he is perfectly capable of turning his imagination, his technology, to free himself from the burden, the inconvenience, and the inadaptability of nourishing the new organism in his own body during the first nine months of its life. It is not in man's nature to accept passively any limitations of nature. His imagination constantly seeks new ways to free himself from it.[20]

But the meaning is muffled. One hardly knows the extent of the suggestion. It is better to go directly to the Chief Engineer of Women's Technology, to the Surgeon-General of the female Armies of Liberation. Ti-Grace Atkinson states the case.

The first step that would have to be taken before we could see exactly what the status of sexual intercourse is as a practice is surely to remove all its institutional aspects: We would have to eliminate the functional aspect. Sexual intercourse would have to cease to be Society's means to population renewal. This change is beginning to be within our grasp with the work now being done on extra-uterine conception and incubation. But the possibilities of this research for the woman's movement have been barely suggested and there would have to be very concentrated research to perfect as quickly as possible this extra-uterine method of pre-natal development so that this could be a truly optional method, at the very least.[21]

They would lift the embryo from that incarcerating womb, handle it with all the care a gourmet offers an

65

oyster as he slips it into his throat, but they would slide it into a tube and then presumably some species of plastic sack with a culture placenta on a petri dish, and a window cut into the bag so that the liberated mother could monitor weekly progress if she wished. The metastasis of technology had proceeded far if it was the women who now respected it most. Extra-uterine gestation was a feat which would yet be applauded by colonies on the moon, and man seemed ready to become a disease which could travel across the stars, while embryos for future use, essential on those trips, would be kept in racks of deepest womb-freeze. Yes, we were coming to the end of that extraordinary long road which had begun with the taking of pills to direct one's mood. It was critical to keep the ego captain of the ship. But Atkinson was ready to go further. Perhaps she was in command of a logic which would not cease.

. . . In order to improve their condition, those individuals who are today defined as women must eradicate their own definition. Women must, in a sense, commit suicide, and the journey from womanhood to a society of individuals is hazardous.

Still further: it did not look as if there would be remission of guilt.

Some psychic relief was achieved by one half the human race at the expense of the other half. Men neatly decimated

Mankind by one half when they took advantage of the
social disability of those Men who bore the burden of the
reproductive process; men invaded the being of those in-
dividuals now defined as functions, or "females," appro-
priated their human characteristics and occupied their
bodies.[22]

If technology was the assertion of men who were not
notably gifted at arts of war or love (and so acquired
their sense of the masculine by daring to work with
forces they did not comprehend), then virility had become a quality blank as plastic, an abstract power over
the employment of techniques. Virility was no longer
to be measured "at the root of the belly where the
phallus rose thick and arching . . . gold-red, vivid"
— no, D. H. Lawrence was obsolete. He who had no
command over modern bodies of technique was out of
it.

Yet if past revolutions had been the attempt of the
exploited to define themselves as men, and present attempts (since power was now technological) were to
achieve command of techniques, then the female revolution, Women's Liberation itself, would have an in-
built tendency to technologize women; what was most
absurd about Atkinson became therefore what was
most seminal about her ideas — women might yet
have to perceive themselves as "Men who bore the

burden of the reproductive process," indeed they would have to if power possessed some intrinsic ability to intensify the masculinization of a human ego. Whatever could be the fruit of the logic?

But kaleidoscopes came on the mind of a victory of women. Would they not rush to cut a bypass into the buttocks of man so that feces might leave by an inlaid tube? The mucus membrane of the anus could then proceed to give all men cunts. They might sew a perma-flesh of sponge and casing on the labia majora with a purse of plastic testicles to pump it full. All the men and all the women would then have phalluses and holes. For certain: they would never fuck themselves — they would just sing praises to the command of a logic which did not cease.

But the PW had obviously come too far. In entering such concepts as women who are Men occupied by other Men, it was obvious that he had jumped from peak to peak of the discussion, and now was isolated in an impossible place, obliged to enter on a to-the-lions romance with Ti-Grace Atkinson and the extra-uterine womb, or else admit defeat, look for rescue from his pinnacle, and begin again. Any attempt to comprehend the oncoming revolution of women which moved too rapidly away from the question of who did the dishes, was in danger of missing the clue to the argument,

which was: what is a man? and what indeed is the
passion to be masculine? Without such a notion, anyone who believed that women could do no worse than
men at delivering us from world crisis and air pollu-
tion would be forced to move inch by inch into General Atkinson's army. For her logic is impeccable, unless the passion to be masculine (at least as it could be
detected in those Men who were born with a phallus)
was something more than a species of preening for the
navel, was, in fact, a passion to be masculine rooted in
the flesh and existence of a Creation deeper than reason. The argument, therefore, had become a hunt, and
the game was no less than the nature of that passion.
The Prizewinner, brought down from Atkinson's peak,
was ready on the literary instant to send out his expedi-
tion. He had found the very Kenya of the subject. It
was the book called *Sexual Politics* by Kate Millett, and
once having read it, he might have chosen that text
even if he had never seen the author's face on *Time* or
been aware of the publishing phenomenon of its appearance, for it was a book as unwittingly obsessed
with the nature of men as a child born blind from birth
might be absorbed in imagining what a landscape was
like. So, if the PW would learn little which was new
about women in the pages of *Sexual Politics*, he could
console himself with having picked up a bit already

from the years of his life and the startling injections of Woman's new writing, enough to know he could not begin to evaluate his relocated view of the ladies until he had reconnoitered his comprehension of men. And there was the land of Millett for a game reserve. Bless her! If it was a chopped-up land with pits and whole gorges of topography missing, still it would take him into the rich terrain occupied by mountains and jungles in the work of D. H. Lawrence, Henry Miller, Jean Genet, and himself. Yes, discovery of the passion to be masculine began with the self. Of course he would use her book — it had twenty-five pages on him!

Yet before he could begin, he recognized with uneasiness that there was country still to be traversed between Atkinson and the land of Millett — all that prior thicket of polemic and concept which revolved about Freud, penis envy, and the virtue or vice of the clitoral orgasm. Sexual theories undulated like belly dancers in every bend.

5

As the rooms in which one made love came to resemble one another (even as a motel room in Hong Kong is a motel room in Dubuque) so sex became currency. Ergo, it was not difficult to envision the single permissive standard as a free market for sex, a species of primitive capitalism where the entrepreneur with the most skill and enterprise and sexual funds could reap the highest profit — the adoration of countless mates and mistresses in that ubiquitous bisexual world where men and women were as interchangeable as coin and cash. Of course, that was yet to come. The single permissive sexual standard was only at the beginning of its era; Great Stud and Angel Queen would still end as junkies in Harlem, or Manson on the page which came first in last year's news. There was a world out there of technology, and it worked to other purpose.

The more he thought about it, the more he saw a profound ambiguity in the single permissive sexual standard. Was it the beginning of the technologizing of sex, or a call from the deep? Before the oncoming free market of sex, capitalism certainly stood parodied as a coward's attempt to displace the fundamental competition of sex over to work, money, family, and church. Yes. It was possible that dread of an open sexual competition had been pervasive enough to throw up civilization itself as the first and largest dike to hold back wild and unruly feminine waters.

Masters and Johnson . . . began treating a series of couples with severe, chronic frigidity or impotence. . . . For the women, none of whom had ever experienced orgasms after five or more years of marriage, treatment consisted of careful training of the husband to use the proper techniques essential to all women and the specific ones required by his wife. . . . Daily sessions were instigated of marital coitus followed by prolonged use of the artificial phallus (three to four hours or more). Thus far, with about fifty women treated, every woman but one responded within three weeks at most and usually within a few days. They began at once to experience intense, multiple orgasms.[23]

The average female with optimal arousal will usually be satisfied with three to five manually-induced orgasms; whereas mechanical stimulation, as with the electric vibrator, is less tiring and induces her to go on to long stimulative sessions of an hour or more during which she may have twenty to fifty consecutive orgasms. She will stop only when totally exhausted.[24]

No doubt the most far reaching hypothesis extrapolated from these biological data is the existence of . . . woman's inability ever to reach complete sexual satiation in the pres-

ence of the most intense, repetitive, orgasmic experiences, no matter how produced. Theoretically, a woman could go on having orgasms indefinitely if physical exhaustion did not intervene.[25]

Should these preliminary findings hold . . . the magnitude of the psychological and social problems facing modern mankind is difficult to contemplate.[26]

If woman would not and could not and soon enough might wish not to be satisfied, so fear of that natural woman must have rested at the heart of the itch to build a civilization. Yes, but why did that woman desire such endless satisfaction? — was it to suck out the juice of the universe, or to conceive a child more mighty than any child yet conceived? A man could spend his life looking to answer the question.

All relevant data from the 12000 to 8000 B.C. period indicate that precivilized woman enjoyed full sexual freedom and was often totally incapable of controlling her sexual drive. Therefore, I propose that one of the reasons for the long delay between the earliest development of agriculture (c. 12000 B.C.) and the rise of urban life and the beginning of recorded knowledge (c. 8000–5000 B.C.) was the ungovernable cyclic sexual drive of women. Not until these drives were gradually brought under control by rigidly enforced social codes could family life become the stabilizing and creative crucible from which modern civilized man could emerge.[27]

The power of moderation in man had triumphed in place of her, and what was moderation but the power of common sense drenched in all its buried paranoia? Since paranoia was also the keen ability to predict a result from a carefully installed cause, so the power of moderation had in its timidity helped to create that technology which would yet stifle the world with its lack of moderation.

Therefore the damnable descent of the PW into the arguments of liberated women was obliged to continue. The mysteries of the feminine orgasm, as revealed by their literature, continued to wash over him. What abuse a man had to take! The counterattack had begun. He read the following passage from *The Sexually Adequate Female* with something close to nostalgia for the pompous Freudian certainties of the Fifties:

. . . Whenever a woman is incapable of achieving an orgasm via coitus, provided her husband is an adequate partner, and [instead] prefers clitoral stimulation to any other form of sexual activity, she can be regarded as suffering from frigidity and requires psychiatric assistance.[28]

That went down nowhere with his Amazonian ideologues.

The facts of female anatomy and sexual response tell a different story. There is only one area for sexual climax, although there are many areas for sexual arousal; that area is the clitoris. All orgasms are extensions of sensation from this area. Since the clitoris is not necessarily stimulated sufficiently in the conventional sexual positions, we are left "frigid." [29]

Nor would they pitch camp there.

All this leads to some interesting questions about conventional sex and our role in it. Men have orgasms essentially by friction with the vagina, not the clitoral area, which is external and not able to cause friction the way penetration does. Women have thus been defined sexually in terms of what pleases men; our own biology has not been properly analyzed. Instead, we are fed the myth of the liberated woman and her vaginal orgasm — an orgasm which in fact does not exist.

What we must do is redefine our sexuality.[30]

Joy was in their delineation of the inferior senses of the vagina against the prides of the clitoris.

The clitoris is a small equivalent of the penis, except for the fact that the urethra does not go through it as in the man's penis. Its erection is similar to the male erection, and the head of the clitoris has the same type of structure and function as the head of the penis. G. Lombard Kelly, in Sexual Feeling in Married Men and Women, *says:*

> "The head of the clitoris is also composed of erectile tissue, and it possesses a very sensitive epithelium or surface covering, supplied with special nerve endings called genital corpuscles,

which are peculiarly adapted for sensory stimulation. . . . No other part of the female generative
tract has such corpuscles."

*The clitoris has no other function than that of sexual
pleasure.*[31]

Whereas, they were quick to point out, the inside of
the vagina, that very interior which according to
Freudian partisans was the precise home of the orgasm, was in fact "like nearly all other internal body
structures, poorly supplied with end organs of touch.
The internal entodermal origin of the lining of the vagina makes it similar in this respect to the rectum and
other parts of the digestive tract." The degree of insen-
sitivity inside the vagina is so high that "among women
who were tested in our gynecologic sample, less than
14% were at all conscious that they had been
touched." [32]

Those specimen women had been tested by Kinsey.
One can conceive of the laboratory conditions, and the
paralysis of all senses which may have sat on the
women, lying there, vagina open, numb as a dead
tooth to that inquiry beneath the probe of the investi-
gator's sterilized eye. Still! Only 14 percent felt a
thing. What a confusion! What a blow to self-esteem
for any man! "The vast majority of women who pre-

tend vaginal orgasm are faking it to," as Ti-Grace Atkinson says, " 'get the job.' " Damn hot spot of a clitoris. What had happened to Blake's most lovely idea
that "Embraces are cominglings from the Head to the
Feet"?

What of his own poor experience? All lies? He felt a
hate for the legions of the vaginally frigid, out there
now with all the pent-up buzzing of a hive of bees,
souped-up pent-up voltage of a clitoris ready to
spring! yes, if there were women who came as if light-
ning bolts had flung their bodies across a bed, were
there not also women who came with the gentlest
squeeze of the deepest walls of the vagina, women
who came every way, even women who seemed never
to come yet claimed they did, and never seemed to
suffer? yes, and women who purred as they came and
women who screamed, women who came as if a finger
had been tickling them down a mile-long street and
women who arrived with the firm frank avowal of a
gentleman shaking hands, yes, if women came in every
variety — one could hardly reach the age of forty, call
it forty-seven, soon to be forty-eight, without knowing
something of that, even the most modest of men could
know something of that — then how to account for the
declaration that vaginal orgasm was myth, and friction
upon the clitoris was the only way an excitation could

discharge? No, he had boobed along like the other men, mind trying to fix a reasonable balance between the dictum that the best of feminine orgasms was vaginal against his experience which seemed to speak of a splurge of orgasms in women which came not so near to being defined, orgasms which spoke back and forth, until Emily Dickinson herself might have cried, "Where the button, who the hole?," orgasms which came from you knew not where. (From Heaven, was the unvoiced hope.) Now the bitter gruel — women came uniquely from the clitoris. That was the word; the rest was lies. Women, went the cry, liberate yourselves from the tyranny of the vagina. It is nothing but a flunky to the men.

Men fear that they will become sexually expendable if the clitoris is substituted for the vagina as the center of pleasure for women. Actually this has a great deal of validity if one considers only the anatomy. The position of the penis inside the vagina, while perfect for reproduction, does not necessarily stimulate an orgasm in women because the clitoris is located externally and higher up. Women must rely upon indirect stimulation in the "normal" position.

Lesbian sexuality could make an excellent case, based upon anatomical data, for the extinction of the male organ. Albert Ellis says something to the effect that a man without a penis can make a woman an excellent lover.

But what was the name of this author? Why, her name was not Shears but Koedt.

Aside from the strictly anatomical reasons why women might equally seek other women as lovers, there is a fear on men's part that women will seek the company of other women on a full, human basis. The establishment of clitoral orgasm as fact would threaten the heterosexual institution. *For it would indicate that sexual pleasure was obtainable from either men or women, thus making heterosexuality not an absolute, but an option. It would thus open up the whole question of* human *sexual relationships beyond the confines of the present male-female role system.*[33]

If the tender concern of this view left a man confronting the clitoris like a twitch before the switch of a dynamo, the recovery of some vanity was not necessarily going to be achieved by any sops thrown him. If there were medical descriptions to puzzle through, the mind's eye had to correlate the draperies of the outer vagina to this Latinate text: ". . . Clitoris, labia minora, and lower third of the vagina function as a single, smoothly integrated unit when traction is placed on the labia by the male organ during coitus. Stimulation of the clitoris is achieved by the rhythmical pulling on the edematous prepuce." [34]

So the vagina had been reinstated, by a third perhaps it had been reinstated, but a man still had to

abandon plump and palpitating upper two-thirds, all
that now condemned to be neuter and nerveless — he
had a glimpse of how Tories reacted when India was
lost.

Was he ready enough for the counterattack? He was
primed in fact to go. He would treat these ladies to a
bit of male irony on the relative comparison of clitoris
to penis, yea, as a pea, a curled anchovy, as a shrimp to
a cucumber — those were dimensions they preferred
to ignore! And was off on a new anger at Woman's
ubiquitous plenitude of orgasms with that plastic
prick, that laboratory dildoe, that vibrator! He would
yet have more to say on the female orgasm than the
ladies had themselves, yes, he would, but his anger
calmed before the little misery of knowing he was not
really unhappy to come across the sweet if liberal sex-
ology of Germaine Greer, the English lecturer from
Warwick U and Upper James St., Golden Square. It
was a sign of age to lean upon the compromises of the
liberal heart.

*The banishment of the fantasy of the vaginal orgasm
is ultimately a service, but the substitution of the clitoral
spasm for genuine gratification may turn out to be a disaster for sexuality. Masters and Johnson's conclusions have
produced some unlooked for side-effects, like the veritable
clitoromania which infects Mette Eiljersen's book, I Ac-*

cuse! *While speaking of women's orgasms as resulting from the "right touches on the button" she condemns sexologists who [denigrate]*

> ". . . the stimulation of the clitoris as part of the prelude to . . . the 'real thing.' What is in fact the 'real thing' for them is completely devoid of sensation for the woman.
> "This is the heart of the matter! Concealed for hundreds of years by humble, shy and subservient women."

Not all the women in history have been humble and subservient to such an extent. It is nonsense to say that a woman feels nothing when a man is moving his penis in her vagina: the orgasm is qualitatively different when the vagina can undulate around the penis instead of a vacancy.[35]

"Qualitatively different." Like blinded Samson, or Oedipus reduced, the pride of a man could bow in gratitude before this restorative crust thrown by the lady Greer why, she would even remark "if the right chain reaction should happen, women might find that the clitoris was more directly involved in intercourse, and could be brought to climax by a less pompous and deliberate way than digital massage," could even go on to such bestowal of equal status as to grant:

Women's continued high enjoyment of sex, which continues after orgasm, observed by men with wonder, is not

*based on the clitoris, which does not respond particularly
well to continued stimulus, but in a general sensual response. If we localize female response in the clitoris we
impose upon women the same limitation of sex which has
stunted the male's response. The male sexual ideal of virility without languor or amorousness is profoundly desolat-
ing: when the release is expressed in mechanical terms it
is sought mechanically. Sex becomes masturbation in the
vagina.*

*Many women who greeted the conclusions of Masters
and Johnson with cries of "I told you so!" and "I am normal!" will feel that this criticism is a betrayal. They have
discovered sexual pleasure after being denied it but the
fact that they have only ever experienced gratification from
clitoral stimulation is evidence for my case, because it is
the index of the desexualization of the whole body, the
substitution of genitality for sexuality.*[36]

It would have been tempting to rush through this
breach in the women's lines with the cry, "You're
guilty once again of the primal crime, you are all as
Eve with your envy of the penis that is not yours!" He
was tempted, for the cry was not without its ring, and
he was raw with listening to the buried raucousness of
female voices.

But there was a difficulty. He did not believe in
penis envy. Unless women were the inheritors of a
curse which passed through the generations of their
sex from the first Garden, it was hard to see why penis

envy must be the spine of the female psyche, no, not hard-core penis envy at the age of four when contemplating a loss of diapers on a naked boy of three.

. . . It would seem that girls are fully cognizant of male supremacy long before they see their brother's penis. It is so much a part of their culture, so entirely present in the favoritism of school and family, in the image of each sex presented to them by all media, religion, and in every model of the adult world they perceive, that to associate it with a boy's distinguishing genital would, since they have learned a thousand other distinguishing sexual marks by now, be either redundant or irrelevant. Confronted with so much concrete evidence of the male's superior status, sensing on all sides the depreciation in which they are held, girls envy not the penis, but only what the penis gives one social pretensions to.[37]

Yes, that was Millett at her best, and penis envy was a slander upon the complexity of the female just so much as pussy envy was a canard on the male, no, it might be more natural to believe that God had established man and woman in some asymmetry of forces which was the life of the aesthetic, man with his penis, woman with her womb — yes, certainly that must be in the conception of the human project if Man (with Woman) loomed large in the works of the Lord.

Filled with such fine and resonating sentiments, the Prisoner was obliged to conclude that the repression of ghetto centuries was to be felt in the cruel and unreasonable pinch of Freud's concepts. What a cramp on philosophy was the castration complex with its insistence that the bottom of all buried fear in man was his fear that the penis would be lost; no, the PW had often been tempted to write in parallel to Millett that fear of losing the penis was not the root of other fears so much as it was the final product of social fears, that one would, for example — let us enjoy the example — not be afraid of a maniacal Amazon in a dark alley so much because one had harbored the terror from the age of three that the penis could be lost at a clip, as from fear that the huge murderess upon one was so dangerous, so voracious, that nothing, not even one's buried prick, was safe; to the contrary, the PW had often thought that the castration complex was more likely to be a trauma which had struck Freud personally, struck him on the instant of his circumcision. No mean trauma. That the first searing, sense-shattering pain after birth should explode on the senses from there, *there!* in *that* region of the body, would be cause enough for later fear of castration. Freud never cared to question the rite of circumcision but we can suspect how his unconscious must have worried the possibility that circumcision was the fastest way to relocate libido from the genitals to the brain and the mouth.

(Which is fuel for every bigot who used to declare New Yorkers were quick-talking and slick, but since circumcision is now fast practice in many a hospital — "They trimmed his little old twig in less time than I could open my gums to say, 'Leave that boy alone,'" moaned the red-neck — the suspicion is reinforced that civilization has appropriated the rite because technology has need of populations whose mental energy predominates over genital, a fat remark! Once stated, it is so full of unhappy mass that one can strain his back trying to remove it from consciousness.)

So the PW was inclined to follow the possibility that Freud had displaced the trauma of his circumcision and thereby had made the grand error of assuming that his unique set of blocks, inhibitions, and inchoate anxieties, plus the field of snarls between his mind and his groin, were the universal castration complex (and indeed his modest sex life gives every indication of whole areas of desire sufficiently cauterized to be thought of as gone and amputated). Yet once deprived of anything like some average use of his genitals, it is not inconceivable Freud made the reasonable error of projecting his envy of other men's penises over to women. In any case, from the best or most unhappy of motives, we have inherited the concept of penis envy. Now, that extraordinary range of hostilities, just and unjust, which a woman can muster toward a man, will be given such a label as penis envy at exactly the moment a male feels he is dealing with a force directly opposed to him and void of love, when a woman is in short acting like a male muscle, or may it be like a male ego? Yet is that penis envy we see then in the hard concerted look of her eye, or is it penis contempt? We are long familiar with male contempt of the pussy and, lately, with pussy envy. Now penis contempt may as well accompany the others, for the look in the woman's eye bemoans the fact she is not a man, since if she were a man, or better still, a woman with command of a phallus entrusted to her, she would know how to use it, God she would know how to use it better than a man, which may not be an unfair portrait of a woman thinking across the gulf of sex: whereas a man is not often ready to explain that a phallus is not a simple instrument but a contradictory, treacherous, all-too-spontaneous sport who is sometimes the expression of a part of oneself not quite under Central Control, indeed often at odds with the will. If this seems odd or exaggerated to women, they can be reminded that in the profound pussy envy of men there is the simple even sentimental suspicion that it is easy to be a woman — one need merely lie back and all Heaven will come into the cunt. Any woman reading such a thought and amusing herself at how far such a simple assumption is removed from those maddening regions of frustration which lie between an open vagina and whole satisfaction may do well to recognize that demands upon a man are conceivably as intricate.

The PW was thereby back again in the enigma of orgasm, and the drear fear of attempting to comprehend it. And if he was not even near understanding his own, how did he think himself qualified to be onto the coming of a woman? Yet if life abounded in mysteries (and he was first with the passion to say yes) it seemed to him comprehension was acquired of the mysterious by the same way one went to faith — by a leap (which perhaps is why he was never able to rid himself of the thought that suicide via jumping from the nineteenth floor was a religious act, could be no less) but we are all immersed in ideas which are extreme — if only to escape the paranoia which sits on those who cling to common sense — so he preferred to believe that the Lord, Master of Existential Reason, was not thus devoted to the absurd as to put the orgasm in the midst of the act of creation without cause of the profoundest sort, for when a man and woman conceive, would it not be best that they be able to see one another for a transcendent instant, as if the soul of what would then be conceived might live with more

light later? A beautiful idea — it will curdle in the air
of its print. Sex is reason, sex is common sense, sex is
ego and prudence and scum on the sheets as the towel
is missed on the pullout, sex is come by your kink, and
freak will I on mine, sex is fifty whips of the clitoris
pinging through with all the authority of a broken
nerve in the tooth, poor middle-class bewildered plain
housewives' libido coming in like an oil well under the
paved-over barnyard of a bewildered cunt, modest
churchgoing women with plastic vibrating dildoe. The
sanction of all science is here, white and sterile phar-
maceutical mass, black as goat dung goes the popping
of the libido on laboratory lane, and the brain is
flushed with the winning adrenaline of ego: "I'm a
middle-aged woman and I came fifty times," yes, the
lady in the lab was the Story of O: women had been
built to come when open — whether tortured or pam-
pered they would come when open, and men could
come when at last they could open, and one could
come out of a cornucopia of choices or from a single
highway deprived of any other exit, but the come was
the mirror to the character of the soul as the soul went
over the hill into the next becoming. What desire had
technology to calibrate this being-within-a-being when
the human was the unit, and the groupings of unit
were blocks of social use? Sexual technology could

best be served by orgasms able to be measured by periodicity and count. Why, then, offer the attentions of theory to orgasms stunted as lives, screwed as mean and fierce and squashed and cramped as the lives of men and women whose history was daily torture, nor contemplate comings as far away as the aria and the hunt and the devil's ice of a dive, orgasms like the collision of a truck, or coming soft as snow, arriving with the riches of a king in costume, or slipping in with the sneaky heat of a slide down slippery slopes. Not technology but the eye of your life looked back at you then. Who would wish to stare into that eye if it was poorer than one's own? No, one had to take the leap without real knowledge, go up and over all of clitoral-medical polemic, go above that debris of the sexual-technical, and land on the statement that a lack of nerves in the upper waters of the vagina had as little to do with fair placement of the real seat of the orgasm as the recognition that gray matter in the skull case of the brain being equally unirrigated by a network of nerves was therefore an indication that the head was not the seat of thought. No, the more remarkable the orgasm, the higher it would fly above the nerve, there in the squeeze of the act, the come might arrive in a dribble or in a transcendental rush, but privates could speak with wires all unattached, even as there was telepathy in preference to the phone.

So the vaginal orgasm was safe — still safe for him at least — held by a net of metaphor suspended from a nonexistent string, but he went on reading with no lack of fear in his heart at the ferocity of these fifty clitoral laboratory orgasms lost by transmission into the plastic ether of some scalded libidinal bile-filled psychosocial air. Where would their message go? For nothing, he believed, was ever wholly lost, no curse, no cry of wasted come. But we are already on to the men, and the passion to be male. Angels and devils are collecting in the embrace at Revolution Hall.

III The Advocate

Y ANY MAJOR LITERARY PERSPECTIVE, the land of Millett is a barren and mediocre terrain, its flora reminiscent of a Ph.D. tract, its roads a narrow argument, and its horizon low. Still, there is a story they tell

of Kate Millett when the winds blow and lamps gutter with a last stirring of the flame. Then, as the skirts of witches go whipping around the wick, they tell how Kate went up to discuss the thesis at her college and a learned professor took issue with her declaration that the wife of the hero Rojack in a work called *An American Dream* had practiced sodomy with husband and lovers.

"No, no," cried the professor. "I know the author, I know him well, I have discussed the scene with him more than once and it is not sodomy she practices, but analingus. It is for that she is killed, since it is a vastly more deranging offense in the mind's eye!"

It is said that Kate turned pale and showed cold sweat upon her skin. But she was not a future leader of millions for nothing, her argument depended on sodomy, and the art of argument was to ignore forever what did not fit; her work appeared with this good passage:

. . . *Here is where one must depend on the forceful role of sodomy in the book, she admits that she has been enjoying this very activity with her new lovers. Now sodomy is a specialty in which our hero takes personal pride. Though he boasts to her face that his mistresses far excel her in this activity, the notion that his wife is committing sodomous adultery is evidently too severe a trial on his patience*

. . . he promptly retaliates by strangling the upstart. As Mrs. Rojack is one of those Celtic sporting women, it is not easy work . . .

Well, it could be said for Kate that she was nothing if not a pug-nosed wit, and that was good, since in literary matters she had not much else. Her lack of fidelity to the material she read was going to be equaled only by her authority in characterizing it — analingus was yes as sodomy — and the yaws of her distortion were nicely hidden by the smudge pots of her indignation. So her land was a foul and dreary place to cross, a stingy country whose treacherous inhabitants (were they the very verbs and phrases of her book?) jeered at difficulties which were often the heart of the matter, the food served at every inn was a can of ideological lard, a grit and granite of thesis-factories turned out aggregates of concept-jargon on every ridge, stacks of such clauses fed the sky with smoke, and musical instruments full of the spirit of nonviolence emitted the sound of flaws and blats. Bile and bubbles of intellectual flatulence coursed in the river, and the bloody ground steamed with the limbs of every amputated quote. Everywhere were signs that men were guilty and women must win.

What then has happened to our promise of a varied

terrain of mountains and jungles, of explorations into
the work of novelists known for their preoccupation
with the needs of men? Has it disappeared altogether,
or is it that any trek across this bog of flatland, swamp,
and grinding sands of prose is no more than a skitter
across a rhetorical skin, a steamy literary webbing
whose underneath, once upturned, reveals another
world, a circus of subterranean attractions which can
be viewed only by digging up each quotation buried
in her book? For each corpse was so crudely assassi-
nated, then so unceremoniously dumped, that the poor
fellows are now as martyrs beneath the sod, and
every shroud is become a phosphorescence of literary lights, a landscape of metaphorical temples. Yet
if we are able to find such a literary world, when entrance requires no less than the resurrection of the
corpses in her graves, what is to be said of her method?
Can she be an honor student in some occult school of
thuggee (now open to the ladies via the pressures of
Women's Liberation)? It is possible. For Kate is the
perfect gun. It is as if she does not know why she kills,
just senses that here the job is ready to be done, and
there the job must be done. It is almost as if some
higher tyrant has fingered the quotes, has said, "They
are getting too close to a little divine sense here —
bury 'em deep in shit, Kate-baby."

Kate-baby nods, goes out. A sawed-off shotgun is her tool. What a blast at Henry Miller:

As all Americans know, the commercial world is a battle-field. When executives are "fucked" by the company, they can retaliate by "fucking" their secretaries. Miller's is "part-nigger" and "so damned pleased to have someone fuck her without blushing," that she can be shared out to the boss's pal Curley. She commits suicide eventually, but in business, "it's fuck or be fucked," Miller observes, pro-viding some splendid insight into the many meanings we attach to the word.

"It's fuck or be fucked," writes Millett, quoting Miller. Except it is not Miller she is quoting — even if she gives him words and puts them in quotation marks. Did an editor discover a discrepancy? There is a footnote: "This is the sense of the passage." But it is not the sense. Miller writes: "We were a merry crew, united in our desire to fuck the company at all costs. And while fucking the company we fucked everything in sight that we could get hold of . . ."[1] — a merry observation, not a bitter one. But Kate's version works more effectively to slip a reader the assumption that Miller is a racist who jeers at his secretary's death: "She commits suicide eventually, but in business, 'it's fuck or be fucked,' Miller observes," although now we know this has not been his observation. In fact, the

97

suicide isn't even mentioned at that point in *Tropic of Capricorn* — it's mentioned twenty-eight pages later in an opposite context where Miller, discovering that the secretary is about to be fired because one of his superiors doesn't want a Negro in the company, comes to her defense, describes her indeed to his superiors as "extremely intelligent and extremely capable." To himself, he thinks, "when she was angry she was magnificent . . ." Miller has begun to fall in love with her. But we may as well enjoy the passage.

I told her quietly that if she were fired I would quit too. She pretended not to believe it at first. I said I meant it, that I didn't care what happened. She seemed to be unduly impressed; she took me by the two hands and she held them very gently, the tears rolling down her cheeks.

That was the beginning of things. I think it was the very next day that I slipped her a note saying that I was crazy about her. She read the note sitting opposite me and when she was through she looked me square in the eye and said she didn't believe it. But we went to dinner again that night and we had more to drink and we danced and while we were dancing she pressed herself against me lasciviously. It was just the time, as luck would have it, that my wife was getting ready to have another abortion. I was telling Valeska about it as we danced. On the way home she suddenly said — "Why don't you let me lend you a hundred dollars?" The next night I brought her home to dinner and I let her hand the wife the hundred dollars.

I was amazed how well the two of them got along. Before the evening was over it was agreed upon that Valeska would come to the house the day of the abortion and take care of the kid. The day came and I gave Valeska the afternoon off. About an hour after she had left I suddenly decided that I would take the afternoon off also. I started toward the burlesque on Fourteenth Street. When I was about a block from the theater I suddenly changed my mind. It was just the thought that if anything happened — if the wife were to kick off — I wouldn't feel so damned good having spent the afternoon at the burlesque. I walked around a bit, in and out of the penny arcades, and then I started homeward.

It's strange how things turn out. Trying to amuse the kid I suddenly remembered a trick my grandfather had shown me when I was a child. You take the dominoes and you make tall battleships out of them; then you gently pull the tablecloth on which the battleships are floating until they come to the edge of the table when suddenly you give a brisk tug and they fall onto the floor. We tried it over and over again, the three of us, until the kid got so sleepy that she toddled off to the next room and fell asleep. The dominoes were lying all over the floor and the tablecloth was on the floor too. Suddenly Valeska was leaning against the table, her tongue halfway down my throat, my hand between her legs. As I laid her back on the table she twined her legs around me. I could feel one of the dominoes under my feet — part of the fleet that we had destroyed a dozen times or more.

At this point, Miller goes off into a reverie about his grandfather and his boyhood (which is his way of protracting the act). A nostalgic reverie follows with memories of photographs in boyhood books, Teddy Roosevelt, San Juan Hill, the *Maine*, Admiral Dewey, Schley and Sampson. Then he writes:

> . . . *We had hardly finished when the bell rang and it was my wife coming home from the slaughterhouse. I was still buttoning my fly as I went through the hall to open the gate. She was as white as flour. She looked as though she'd never be able to go through another one. We put her to bed and then we gathered up the dominoes and put the tablecloth back on the table.*

Well, he has certainly fucked her, and fucked her while his wife is having an abortion, and left us with an image of a white man making love to a black woman while thinking of San Juan Hill, and one hundred twenty-one pages later he has not so much loaned her as lost her to his friend Curley, but the sense we have been given by Millett of a boss using his black secretary shamelessly, and jeering at her suicide, is warped. "She was so damned pleased to have someone fuck her without blushing," is in context the bitter and painful remark of a man who felt some love for a woman who when alive "was picked clean too, by the human worms who have no respect for anything which has a different tint, a different odor."

That last note is, of course, vintage. Only a comic
liberal would speak today of respect for people with
different tints, but *Tropic of Capricorn* came out in
1939 and is about the Twenties when it was still radical to believe whites and blacks could make love together, the work of Miller is in fact a Baedeker to the
remarkable sexuality of the Twenties, and one would
expect in a book called *Sexual Politics,* which contains
a part titled "The Sexual Revolution, First Phase:
1830–1930," that much would be made of the Twenties, and the work of Miller in relation to it. But "Sexual Revolution, First Phase: 1830–1930," while it in-
cludes nothing less than a brief history of feminism
plus a view of nineteenth-century attitudes toward
women in the work of the Brontës, Mill, Ruskin, Meredith, Hardy, Wilde, and Engels, is egregiously mis-
titled, since there is nothing in it from 1900 to 1930,
nothing of the First World War and the Twenties,
nothing of Fitzgerald, Aleister Crowley, and Caresse
Crosby, nothing of Prohibition, surrealism, Daisy
Buchanan, Brett Ashley, Hollywood, jazz, or the
Charleston, not a word from 1920 to 1930, a decade
conceivably as interesting in the emancipation of
women as any other ten years since the decline of
Rome. But such an inclusion might have called for another hundred pages, which conceivably Millett didn't

have in her head. The Twenties are a thicket for any thesis-monger with an ax. That may be why Millett never once looks at Miller as some wandering troubadour of the Twenties who carried the sexual revolution through the cities of the New World and the Old, no, Miller has been labeled a "counterrevolutionary sexual politician," he belongs to that tidy part of her thesis which will neatly see 1930 to 1960 as a time of sexual counterrevolution. She would hardly be ready, plans drawn, subdivisions staked and sold, to put up with the thundering horror that Miller is an archetype of the man of the Twenties, is indeed the true sexual revolutionary if we are willing to grant that any equivalent figure of the Renaissance would by that measure also be a revolutionary, since no revolution ever picks up momentum without a profound change in the established consciousness of the time. Just as the Renaissance was a period in which men dared, as perhaps never before in history, to allow themselves to pursue the line of their thought and embark on exploration with the idea that such activities were good and valid in themselves and so did not have to be initiated with external blessing or forced to scurry under the shadow of inviolable taboo, but rather the world was a theater, and nature a laboratory open to the adventurer with an inquiring mind — so the Twenties were a species of sexual renaissance where man emerged from the long medieval night of Victorian sex with its perversions, hypocrisies, and brothel dispensations, and set out to explore not the world, but himself, not man of Victorian reason with his buried sexual pocket, but man as himself, Henry Miller, with his brain and his balls in the intimate and continuing dialogue of his daily life, which meant that one followed the line of one's sexual impulse without a backward look at what was moral, responsible, or remotely desirable for society, that one set out to feed one's cock (as man from the Renaissance had set out to feed his brain) and since the effort was pioneer in the very real way that no literary man with the power to shift consciousness had ever given that much attention before to the vagaries and outright contradictions of a stiff prick without a modicum of conscience, no one had ever dared to assume that such a life might be as happy and amusing as the next, that the paganism of a big-city fucker had its own balance, and such a man could therefore wage an all-out war to storm the mysteries with his phallus as a searchlight because all sexual experience was valid if one looked at it clearly and no fuck was in vain, well, it was a sexual renaissance sure enough, and it depended on a rigorous even a delighted honesty in portraying the detail of one's faults, in writing without shit, which is to say writing with the closest examination of one's own. Miller was a true American spirit. He knew that in a nation of transplants and weeds the best was always next to the worst, and right after shit comes Shinola. It was all equal to him because he understood that it is never equal — in the midst of heaven a hole, and out of the slimy coruscated ridiculous comes a pearl; he is a demon at writing about bad fucks with all the gusto he gives to good ones, no fuck is in vain — the air may prove most transcendent at the edge of the vomit, or if not, then the nausea it produces can give birth to an otherwise undiscovered project as the mind clears out of its vertigo. So he dives into the sordid, portrays men and women as they have hardly been painted before, a girl having her period in the middle of an orgy, cock, balls, knees, thighs, cunt, and belly in a basting of blood, then soap and towels, a round of good-byes — a phrase or two later he is off on the beginning of a ten-page description of how he makes love to his wife which goes through many a mood, he will go right down to the depths, no cellar has maggots or rats big enough to frighten him, he can even write about the whipped-out flayed heel-ground end of his own desire, about fucking when too exhausted to fuck, and come up with a major metaphor. Let it be introduced by Kate Millett:

One memorable example of sex as a war of attrition waged upon economic grounds is the fifteen-franc whore whom Miller and his friend Van Norden hire in the Paris night and from whom, despite their own utter lack of appetite and her exhaustion from hunger, it is still necessary to extort the price.

Let us see what Millett is talking about. She seems to have price confused with product. Here is Miller.

And then she commences a hard luck story, about the hospital and the back rent and the baby in the country. But she doesn't overdo it. She knows that our ears are stopped; but the misery is there inside her, like a stone, and there's no room for any other thoughts. She isn't trying to make an appeal to our sympathies — she's just shifting this big weight inside her from one place to another. I rather like her. I hope to Christ she hasn't got a disease.

In the room she goes about her preparations mechanically. "There isn't a crust of bread about by any chance?" she inquires, as she squats over the bidet. Van Norden laughs at this. "Here, take a drink," he says, shoving a bottle at her. She doesn't want anything to drink; her stomach's already on the bum, she complains.

"That's just a line with her," says Van Norden. "Don't let her work on your sympathies. Just the same, I wish she'd talk about something else. How the hell can you get up any passion when you've got a starving cunt on your hands?" [2]

Up to this point, Kate's description has been a reasonable summary. Now she goes on with:

As sex, or rather "cunt," is not only merchandise but a monetary specie, Miller's adventures read like so many victories for sharp practice, carry the excitement of a full ledger, and operate on the flat premise that quantity is quality.

"How the hell can you get up any passion when you have a starving cunt on your hands?" We are installed on the heights of chivalry. Can any author ever recover from this point? But Miller is following the logic where it leads — out of the deepest dungeons will the logic of cock lead him to the towers of metaphor.

Precisely! We haven't any passion either of us. And as for her, one might as well expect her to produce a diamond necklace as to show a spark of passion. But there's the fifteen francs and something has to be done about it. It's like a state of war: the moment the condition is precipitated nobody thinks about anything but peace, about getting it over with. And yet nobody has the courage to lay down his arms, to say, "I'm fed up with it . . . I'm through." No, there's fifteen francs somewhere, which nobody gives a damn about any more and which nobody is going to get in the end anyhow, but the fifteen francs is like the primal cause of things and rather than listen to one's own voice, rather than walk out on the primal cause, one surrenders to the situation, one goes on butchering and butchering and the more cowardly one feels the more heroically does he behave . . .

It's exactly like a state of war — I can't get it out of my head. The way she works over me, to blow a spark of passion into me, makes me think what a damned poor soldier I'd be if I was ever silly enough to be trapped like this and dragged to the front. I know for my part that I'd surrender everything, honor included, in order to get out of the mess. I haven't any stomach for it, and that's all there is to it. But she's got her mind set on the fifteen francs and if I don't want to fight about it she's going to make me fight. But you can't put fight into a man's guts if he hasn't any fight in him.

Victories for sharp practice? Excitement of a full ledger?

Van Norden seems to have a more normal attitude about it. He doesn't care a rap about the fifteen francs either now; it's the situation itself which intrigues him. It seems to call for a show of mettle — his manhood is involved. The fifteen francs are lost, whether we succeed or not. There's something more involved — not just manhood perhaps, but will. It's like a man in the trenches again: he doesn't know any more why he should go on living, because if he escapes now he'll only be caught later, but he goes on just the same, and even though he has the soul of a cockroach and has admitted as much to himself, give him a gun or a knife or even just his bare nails, and he'll go on slaughtering and slaughtering, he'd slaughter a million men rather than stop and ask himself why.

As I watch Van Norden tackle her, it seems to me that I'm looking at a machine whose cogs have slipped. Left to themselves, they could go on this way forever, grinding and slipping, without ever anything happening. Until a hand shuts the motor off. The sight of them coupled like a pair of goats without the least spark of passion, grinding and grinding away for no reason except the fifteen francs, washes away every bit of feeling I have except the inhuman one of satisfying my curiosity. The girl is lying on the edge of the bed and Van Norden is bent over her like a satyr with his two feet solidly planted on the floor. I am sitting on a chair behind him, watching their movements with a cool, scientific detachment; it doesn't matter to me if it should last forever. It's like watching one of those crazy machines which throw the newspaper out, millions and billions and trillions of them with their meaningless headlines. The machine seems more sensible, crazy as it is, and more fascinating to watch, than the human beings and the events which produced it. My interest in Van Norden and the girl is nil; if I could sit like this and watch every single performance going on at this minute all over the world my interest would be even less than nil. I wouldn't be able to differentiate between this phenomenon and the rain falling or a volcano erupting. As long as that spark of passion is missing there is no human significance in the performance. The machine is better to watch. And these two are like a machine which has slipped its cogs. It needs the touch of a human hand to set it right. It needs a mechanic.

I get down on my knees behind Van Norden and I examine the machine more attentively. The girl throws her head on one side and gives me a despairing look. "It's no use," she says. "It's impossible." Upon which Van Norden sets to work with renewed energy, just like an old billy goat. He's such an obstinate cuss that he'll break his horns rather than give up. And he's getting sore now because I'm tickling him in the rump.

"For God's sake, Joe, give it up! You'll kill the poor girl."

"Leave me alone," he grunts. "I almost got it in that time."

But it is just this last fillip of male humor, that fat tone of the farmer working his bull into the calf, the pride of men able to get their hands in the short hair which enrages Millett most, blinds her with such anger that she misses the point Miller will make in another few lines — the quintessential point that lust when it fails is a machine.

You can get over a cunt and work away like a billy goat until eternity; you can go to the trenches and be blown to bits; nothing will create that spark of passion if there isn't the intervention of a human hand. Somebody has to put his hand into the machine and let it be wrenched off if the cogs are to mesh again. Somebody has to do this without hope of reward, without concern over the fifteen francs . . .

But again, what sort of victory is this for sharp practice? The only sharp practice is in her assessment of the passage. Literary lawyers cannot do criticism, they can only write briefs, and Kate holds court in the land of Millett. Poor Henry. He has spent his literary life exploring the watershed of sex from that uncharted side which goes by the name of lust and it is an epic work for any man; over the centuries, most of the poets of the world have spent their years on the other side; they wrote of love. But lust is a world of bewildering dimensions, for it is that power to take over the ability to create and convert it to a force. Curious force. Lust exhibits all the attributes of junk. It dominates the mind and other habits, it appropriates loyalties, generalizes character, leaches character out, rides on the fuel of almost any emotional gas — whether hatred, affection, curiosity, even the pressures of boredom — yet it is never definable because it can alter to love or be as suddenly sealed from love, indeed the more intense lust becomes, the more it is indefinable, the line of the ridge between lust and love is where the light is first luminous, then blinding, and the ground remains unknown. Henry, a hairy prospector, red eye full of lust, has wandered these ridge lines for the years of his literary life, getting to know the mosquitoes by name down in every swamp and calling to the ozones of the highest lust on many a cloud-covered precipice. While cunts are merely watering places for that lust, boscage, fodder, they are also, no matter how despised — it is the private little knowledge of lust — that indispensable step closer to the beyond, so old Priapus the ram admits, "perhaps a cunt, smelly though it may be, is one of the prime symbols for the connection between all things."

He has slipped the clue across. Here is a motive to the lust that drives a man to scour his balls and his back until he is ready to die from the cannonading he has given his organs, the deaths through which he has dragged some futures of his soul, it is a clue which all but says that somewhere in the insane passions of all men is a huge desire to drive forward into the seat of creation, grab some part of that creation in the hands, sink the cock to the hilt, sink it into as many hilts as will hold it; for man is alienated from the nature which brought him forth, he is not like woman in possession of an inner space which gives her link to the future, so he must drive to possess it, he must if necessary come close to blowing his head off that he may possess it. "Perhaps a cunt, smelly though it may be, is one of the prime symbols for the connection between all things."

Of course Kate will put it in somewhat less commendatory fashion:

In the case of the two actual women . . . who appear in Miller's world amidst its thousand floozie caricatures, personality and sexual behavior is so completely unrelated that, in the sexual episodes where they appear, any other names might have been conveniently substituted. For the purpose of every bout is the same: a demonstration of the hero's self-conscious detachment before the manifestations of a lower order of life. During an epic encounter with

Mara, the only woman he ever loved, Miller is as clinical as he was toward Ida; Mara just as grotesque:

> "And on this bright and slippery gadget Mara twisted like an eel. She wasn't any longer a woman in heat, she wasn't even a woman; she was just a mass of indefinable contours wriggling and squirming like a piece of fresh bait seen upside down through a convex mirror in a rough sea.
>
> "I had long ceased to be interested in her contortions; except for the part of me that was in her I was cool as a cucumber and remote as the Dog Star . . .
>
> "Towards dawn, Eastern Standard Time, I saw by the frozen condensed-milk expression about the jaw that it was happening. Her face went through all the metamorphoses of early uterine life, only in reverse. With the last dying spark it collapsed like a punctured bag, the eyes and nostrils smoking like toasted acorns in a slightly wrinkled lake of pale skin."

Mouthpiece for a corporate body of ideas, Kate has neglected to state that it is another of Miller's descriptions of the worst of fucks, of a marathon of lust-fuck in which he is fixed, which he loathes. It is, precisely, not typical of the act with Mara, but then here is what he wrote just before the passage she quotes:

When I returned to resume the ordeal my cock felt as if it were made of old rubber bands. I had absolutely no more feeling at that end; it was like pushing a piece of stiff suet down a drain-pipe. What's more, there wasn't another charge left in the battery; if anything was to happen now it would be in the nature of gall and leathery worms or a drop of pus in a solution of thin pot cheese. What surprised me was that it continued to stand up like a hammer; it had lost all the appearance of a sexual implement; it looked disgustingly like a cheap gadget from the five and ten cent store, like a bright-colored piece of fishing tackle minus the bait. And on this bright and slippery gadget Mara twisted like an eel.[3]

It is curious that she will find these extraordinary descriptions of the horrors of near-dead ice-cold bang-it-out fucking to be odious, as if she is the Battling Annie of some new prudery, yet Kate is still the clarion call for that single permissive sexual standard where a man's asshole is the democratic taxpaying equivalent of any vagina. Of course, it is denigration of woman she protests, the reduction of woman to object, to meat for the cock, woman as a creature who can tune the prick and allow man to adjust his selfish antenna toward the connection of all things, it is the lack of Miller's regard for woman as a person which she claims to abhor, yet in another part of the land of Millett, on page 117 of *Sexual Politics*, Kate is all but invoking praise for Masters and Johnson because they "prove that the female sexual cycle is capable of multiple orgasms in quick succession, each of which is analogous to the detumescence, tumescence, ejaculation, and loss of erection in the male. With proper stimulation, a woman is capable of multiple orgasms in quick succession," she repeats, hardly able to contain herself, and goes on to sing of the clitoris as "the organ specific to sexuality in the human female," yes, the red-hot button of lust gets its good marks here, even as she approves by implication of the methods used to make the Masters and Johnson study, yes, those vibrators and plastic dildoes are honorable adjuncts of sexo-scientific endeavor as opposed to the foul woman-hating billy-goat bulb of old Henry. What a scum of hypocrisy on the surface of her thought, bold sexual revolutionary who will not grant that such a revolution if it comes will have more to do with unmanageable metamorphoses between love and lust than some civilized version of girls-may-hold-hands-in-the-suburbs. It is the horror of lust, and yet its justification, that wild as a blind maniac it still drives toward the creation, it witnesses such profound significations as, "Her face went through all the metamorphoses of early uterine life, only in reverse." And the clue again is upon us of that moment of transcendence when the soul stands in the vault of the act and the coming is its mirror. Yes, even fifty clitoral comes in white-hot vibrating laboratory lust is a mirror (if only of the outer galaxies of nausea) but it is not love but lust, good old scientific lust, pure as the lust in the first fierce fart of the satyr.

How Kate hates old Henry for this: that he dares to be an energetic scientist but is without a smock, that he does his lab work out of the lab, and yet is so scientific that his amours are as case histories. "Personality and sexual behavior is so completely unrelated that . . . any other names might have been conveniently substituted." How she bangs away at him! "Miller is a compendium of American sexual neuroses," says lab assistant Kate; Miller articulates "the disgust, the contempt, the hostility, the violence, and the sense of filth with which our . . . masculine sensibility surrounds sexuality." "Sheer fantasy . . . exploitative character . . . juvenile egotism . . . brutalized adolescence . . . anxiety and contempt . . . masturbatory revery . . . utter impersonality . . . cruelty and contempt . . . humiliating and degrading . . . sadistic will . . . gratified egotism . . . total abstraction . . . arrested adolescence . . . cultural homosexuality . . . compulsive heterosexual activity . . . authoritarian arrangements . . . absolute license . . . truly obscene ruthlessness . . . virulent sexism . . . a childish fantasy of power . . ." Conceive of these items of abuse, alive as nerves. They twitch in every paragraph for twenty pages. What an apostle for nonviolence is the lady.

Yet the irony is that a case can be brought against Miller. He is so completely an Old Master at his best (he is, in fact, the only Old Master we have) that the failure of the later works to surpass the early ones is a loss everywhere, to Miller, to literature, to us, to all of us. For he captured something in the sexuality of men as it had never been seen before, precisely that it was man's sense of awe before woman, his dread of her position one step closer to eternity (for in that step were her powers) which made men detest women, revile them, humiliate them, defecate symbolically upon them, do everything to reduce them so one might dare to enter them and take pleasure of them. "His shit don't smell like ice cream either," says a private of a general in a novel, and it is the cry of an enlisted man whose ego needs equality to breathe. So do men look to destroy every quality in a woman which will give her the powers of a male, for she is in their eyes already armed with the power that she brought them forth, and that is a power beyond measure — the earliest etchings of memory go back to that woman between whose legs they were conceived, nurtured, and near strangled in the hours of birth. And if women were also born of woman, that could only compound the awe, for out of that process by which they had come in, so would something of the same come out of them; they were installed in the boxes-within-boxes of the universe, and man was only a box, all detached. So it is not unnatural that men, perhaps a majority of men, go through the years of their sex with women in some compound detachment of lust which will enable them to be as fierce as any female awash in the great ocean of the fuck, for as it can appear to the man, great forces beyond his measure seem to be calling to the woman then.

That was what Miller saw, and it is what he brought back to us: that there were mysteries in trying to explain the extraordinary fascination of an act we can abuse, debase, inundate, and drool upon, yet the act repeats an interest — it draws us toward obsession, as if it is the mirror of how we approach God through our imperfections, *Hot,* full of the shittiest lust. In all of his faceless characterless pullulating broads, in all those cunts which undulate with the movements of eels, in all those clearly described broths of soup and grease and marrow and wine which are all he will give us of them — their cunts are always closer than their faces — in all the indignities of position, the humiliation of situation, and the endless revelations of women as pure artifacts of farce, asses all up in the air, still he screams his barbaric yawp of utter adoration for the power and the glory and the grandeur of the female in the universe, and it is his genius to show us that this power can survive any context or any abuse.

Let us relax a moment on the moralisms of Millett.

They are not only pushovers, they are puppets. Speaking boy to boy about another "fuck," Miller remarks, "I moved her around like one of those legless toys which illustrate the principle of gravity." Total victory is gratuitous insult; the pleasure of humiliating the sexual object appears to be far more intoxicating than sex itself. Miller's protégé, Curley, is an expert at inflicting this sort of punishment, in this instance, on a woman whom both men regard as criminally overambitious, disgracefully unaware she is only cunt:

"He took pleasure in degrading her. I could scarcely blame him for it, she was such a prim, priggish bitch in her street clothes. You'd swear she didn't own a cunt the way she carried herself in the street. Naturally, when he got her alone, he made her pay for her highfalutin' ways. He went at it cold-bloodedly. 'Fish it out!' he'd say, opening his fly a little. 'Fish it out with your tongue!' . . . once she got the taste of it in her mouth, you could do anything with her. Sometimes he'd stand her on her hands and push her around the room that way, like a wheelbarrow. Or else he'd do it dog fashion, and while she groaned and squirmed he'd nonchalantly light a cigarette and blow the smoke between her legs. Once he played her a dirty trick doing it that way. He had worked her up to such a state that she was beside herself. Anyway, after he had almost polished the ass off her with his back-scuttling he pulled out for a second, as though to cool his cock off . . . . and shoved a big long carrot up her twat."

The last sentence was supposed to read: "He pulled out for a second, as though to cool his cock off, and then very slowly and gently he shoved a big long carrot up her twat." Millett obviously had not wished to weaken her indictment by qualifying the force of the shove — that was where she once again lost Miller. His work dances on the line of his dialectic. But Millett hates every evidence of the dialectic. She has a mind like a flatiron, which is to say a totally masculine mind. A hard-hat has more curves in his head. Look how the hideousness of the description as Millett has excerpted it is given other nuances by what immediately follows.

. . . *Very slowly and gently he shoved a big long carrot up her twat. "That, Miss Abercrombie," he said, "is a sort of Doppelgänger to my regular cock," and with that he unhitches himself and yanks up his pants. Cousin Abercrombie was so bewildered by it all that she let out a tremendous fart and out tumbled the carrot. At least, that's how Curley related it to me. He was an outrageous liar, to be sure, and there may not be a grain of truth in the yarn, but there's no denying that he had a flair for such tricks.*

THE PRISONER OF SEX

As for Miss Abercrombie and her high-tone Narragansett ways, well, with a cunt like that one can always imagine the worst.

A page later, the dialectic has whipped him clear over to a description of the "best fuck" he ever had, and here the statement of the case is pure Henry, for the girl "was a deaf-mute who had lost her memory, and with the loss of memory she had lost her frigidaire, her curling irons, her tweezers and handbag. She was even more naked than a fish . . . and she was even slipperier. . . . It was dubious at times whether I was in her or she in me." He is in heaven. A cornucopia of encomiums inundate us. Never has he stated his case better.

She just stood there quietly and as I slid my hand up her legs she moved one foot a little to open her crotch a bit more. I don't think I ever put my hand into such a juicy crotch in all my life. It was like paste running down her legs, and if there had been any billboards handy I could have plastered up a dozen or more. After a few moments, just as naturally as a cow lowering its head to graze, she bent over and put it in her mouth. I had my whole four fingers inside her, whipping it up to a froth. Her mouth was stuffed full and the juice pouring down her legs. Not a word out of us, as I say. Just a couple of quiet maniacs working away in the dark like gravediggers. It was a fucking Paradise and I knew it, and I was ready and willing to fuck my brains away if necessary. She was probably the

*best fuck I ever had. She never once opened her trap —
not that night, nor the next night, nor any night. She'd
steal down like that in the dark, soon as she smelled me
there alone, and plaster her cunt all over me. It was an
enormous cunt, too, when I think back on it. A dark, subterranean labyrinth fitted up with divans and cosy corners
and rubber teeth and syringas and soft nestles and eider-
down and mulberry leaves. I used to nose in like the soli-
tary worm and bury myself in a little cranny where it was
absolutely silent, and so soft and restful that I lay like a
dolphin on the oyster banks. A slight twitch and I'd be in
the Pullman reading a newspaper or else up an impasse
where there were mossy round cobblestones and little
wicker gates which opened and shut automatically. Sometimes it was like riding the shoot-the-shoots, a steep plunge
and then a spray of tingling sea crabs, the bulrushes sway-
ing feverishly and the gills of tiny fishes lapping against
me like harmonica stops. In the immense black grotto there
was a silk-and-soap organ playing a predaceous black
music. When she pitched herself high, when she turned
the juice on full, it made a violaceous purple, a deep mulberry stain like twilight, a ventriloqual twilight such as
dwarfs and cretins enjoy when they menstruate. It made
me think of cannibals chewing flowers, of Bantus running
amuck, of wild unicorns rutting in rhododendron beds.
. . . It was one cunt out of a million, a regular Pearl of the
Antilles. . . . In the broad Pacific of sex she lay, a gleam-
ing silver reef surrounded with human anemones, human
starfish, human madrepores.*[4]

But Henry won't be allowed to rest for long. Squirt-
bomb at the ready, Millett is laying for him. Some-

thing in the fling of the imagination is odious as a
water bug to her.

*Throughout the description one not only observes a vulgar
opportunistic use of Lawrence's hocus pocus about blank-
ing out in the mind in order to attain "blood consciousness,"
but one also intuits how both versions of the idea are
haunted by a pathological fear of having to deal with another and complete human personality. . . . One is made
very aware here that in the author's scheme the male is
represented not only by his telepathic instrument, but by
mind, whereas the perfect female is a floating metonomy,
pure cunt, completely unsullied by human mentality.*

But why is Kate now so prim? Doesn't the single
permissive sexual standard offer depersonalization via
the wallop-and-suck of the orgy? Kate is reminiscent
of one of those nice-nellie scourges who used to tyran-
nize the back pages of the *New York Times Book Review*, yes, it is as if Miller deprives her of the right to
have a mind by so splendiferous a description of the
cunt, yes, just as any hard-working intellectual in the
1950's was livid at the intimation that some blacks
might have more genital orientation than Freud had
prescribed for the human lot, so is Millett now properly incensed. Stretched with every adrenaline of over-
kill, her mind next to rigid with fear that women might
have some secret but fundamental accommodation to

Miller's lust that brings them into just such absurd positions, she is therefore always missing the point of her case, she is always pushing into that enforced domain of equality where the sexes, she would declaim, "are inherently in everything alike, save reproductive systems, secondary sexual characteristics, orgasmic capacity and genetic and morphological structure. Perhaps the only thing they can uniquely exchange is semen and transudate." Good laboratory assistant Kate. She is a technologist who drains all the swamps only to discover that the ecological balance has been savaged. She is also one of those minds, totalitarian to the core, which go over to hysteria, abuse (and liquidation at the end of the road) whenever they are forced to build their mind on anything more than a single premise. The real case against Miller is not that he is all wrong, and cocks and cunts are no more than biological details on human beings so that we are even unable to distinguish semen from transudate when suffering from a cold, no, the real case is that Miller is right, yet Ibsen's Nora is also right when she says, "I have another duty, just as sacred. . . . My duty to myself. . . . I believe that before everything else I'm a human being — just as much as you are . . . or at any rate, I shall try to become one." What have we not lost in his novels that there will be never a character like Nora to stand against his men? For it is our modern experience that men filled with every appreciation of sex and women's rights encounter women with an equal appreciation, and the war still continues with what new permutations only a novelist can begin to explore since the novelist is the only philosopher who works with emotions which are at the very edge of the word system, and so is out beyond the scientists, doctors, psychologists, even — if he is good enough — the best of his contemporaries who work at philosophy itself. If it is easy to mock him when, like Miller, he comes close to stumbling off the end of the word system, we know his best and wildest ideas will become the ones most quickly attacked by literary technologists like Millett since such ideas lend themselves to confetti-making in ideological mincers. Miller, a hero twice, to take up writing late and to take it up by writing books he could think no one would ever publish, a writer with the individuality of a giant, was still so lacerated by the loneliness of his midnight concepts that his later works often thin out into subtle parodies of the earlier ones, and he finally hooks his moon-anchor onto what has become for us the same old literary fields of flesh and cunt. The knowledge of our age is different. Those fields are an endless treasure to him, but we have the problem of our contemporary love, and so can only tip our hat, we are looking for an accommodation of the sexes, whereas he calls out for an antagonism — "the eternal battle with woman sharpens our resistance, develops our strength, enlarges the scope of our cultural achievements." Yes, he cries out to us, "the loss of sex polarity is part and parcel of the larger disintegration, the reflex of the soul's death and coincident with the disappearance of great men, great causes, great wars." The ram wandering the ridges has come back as a prophet, and the tablets are in his hands. "Put woman back in her rightful place."

But the men moving silently in all retreat pass the prophet by. It is too late to know if he is right or wrong. The women have breached an enormous hole in the line, and the question is only how far back the men must go before they are ready to establish a front. Confusion is at the crossroads. Will D. H. Lawrence have to be surrendered as well?

2

Sometimes the Prisoner thought women had begun to withdraw respect from men about the time pregnancy lost its danger. For once Semmelweis uncovered the cause of puerperal fever, and the doctor could take over from the midwife, once anesthesia, antiseptics, obstetrics, and delivery by fluorescent light were able to replace boiling water, the lamp by the bed, and the long drum roll of labor, then women began to be insulated from the dramatic possibility of a fatal end. If that had once been a possibility real enough for them to look at their mate with eyes of love or eyes of hate but know their man might yet be the agent of their death, conceive then of the lost gravity of the act, and the diminishment of man from a creature equally mysterious to woman (since he could introduce a creation to her which could yet be her doom) down to the fellow who took lessons on how to satisfy his wife from Masters and Johnson and bowed out to the vibrations of his superior, a vibrator (which, reminiscent of all the power concentrated by corporations in the plastic products of every supermart, had obviously the virility to ring the ladies' disembodied case-history buzzer). Enough! The case has been made for the third time, and can rest. It is, like all argument, an exaggeration. What is more to the point is Millett's remark that "the sexes are inherently in everything alike save reproductive systems," etc.

"Good sister Kate," would reply any lady from the centuries before, "reproductive systems are better than half of it!" and could have been right, for how much will impress us more than the danger of our death? But technology, by extending man's power over nature, reduced him before women; Millett's remark is no longer absurd — it has become the summary of a line of thought which looks to prove that differences between men and women have been exaggerated, are cultural, are shaped by the condition that humans-with-phalluses generally grow up in a masculine culture, and humans-with-vaginas in a feminine milieu, thereby exaggerating the differences. Even before they could speak, their separation was imprinted by the way they were handled, whether ruggedly or maidenly, how sentimentally spoken to, "Hiya, guy! . . . Sweet little girl," and in the language they were soon to learn were numberless indications to shape their consciousness in such ways as to make them more masculine as boys, more feminine as girls. (And indeed, since English had no gender for its nouns, the thought occurred that feminism might have originated in Eng-

land and America precisely because the conditioning
to be masculine or feminine was less implanted in our
language.) Culture had obviously created some of the
polarity of men and women, enough to embolden Millett to say, "Whatever the real differences may be, we
are not likely to know them until the sexes are treated
differently, that is alike." Yet, by every evidence of
style, the sexes were already growing similar, for
whether equipped with phallus or vagina, they came
accoutered in pants and long hair, and such unisex had
been incubating for more than a little while.

*As a student in a graduate class at Harvard, some years
ago, I was a member of a seminar which was asked to
identify which of two piles of a clinical test, the TAT, had
been written by males, and which of the two piles had been
written by females. Only four students out of twenty identi-
fied the piles correctly, and this was after one and a half
months of intensively studying the differences between men
and women. Since this result is below chance, that is, this
result would occur by chance about four out of a thousand
times, we may conclude that there is finally a consistency
here; students are judging knowledgeably within the context of psychological teaching about the differences between men and women; the teachings themselves are
simply erroneous.*[5]

Or was it possible that women had come to identify
themselves with qualities the culture called male, and

so had begun to give answers more manly than the men? But then the Prisoner had also to take into account that "the ability of judges, chosen for their clinical expertise, to distinguish male heterosexuals from male homosexuals on the basis of three widely used clinical projective tests — the Rorschach, the TAT, and the MAP, *was no better than chance.*" [6] Latent homosexuality had become as responsive to test questions as overt, a way of concluding that by any psychic measure heterosexuals were as homosexual already as the homosexuals. Either that, or such qualities as masculine and feminine, heterosexual and homosexual, did not exist in any way we understood them. How natural then for Millett to push past the argument that sex was not so much in the organs as the mind, on to the point that "one must really go further and urge a dissemination to members of each sex of those socially desirable traits previously confined to one or the other while eliminating the bellicosity or excessive passivity useless in either." The remark opened the door to eugenics, and beyond was the stuff of experimental control in the extra-uterine womb. It was the measure of the liberal technologist and the Left totalitarian that they exhibited the social lust to make units of people, a cerebral passion reminiscent of the early days of civil liberties when the liberals who knew least about blacks were most eager to insist that there were only environmental differences between Negroes and whites, and it was the blacks who had finally to emphasize "we were Black before we were born."[7] Nonetheless the evidence could not be ignored that men and women appeared to be biologically more similar than the Prisoner had yet recognized. While Greer could offer the happy information that the "degree of distinguishability between the sexes can vary from something so tiny as to be almost imperceptible to a degree of difference so great that scientists remained for a long time ignorant of the fact that species classified as distinct were in fact male and female of the same species,"[8] still, by all accounts, every mammal, male or female, lived for its first embryonic weeks in the female state, which is to say we all began as females. Only in the second month did the action of the hormone androgen move human embryos with *y* chromosomes over into development as males.

Up to the seventh week the foetus shows no sexually differentiated characteristics, and when sexual development begins it follows a remarkably similar pattern in both sexes. The clitoris and the head of the penis look very alike at first, and the urethra develops as a furrow in both sexes. In boys, the scrotum forms out of the genital swelling, in girls, the labia.[9]

Yes, the similarities in embryo were profound. For if gonads were removed from a female embryo before the first six weeks, she would still grow into a normal female, she would even go through all the regular changes of puberty if, in the absence of the excised ovaries, hormones were fed her. But if the fetal gonads were excised from an embryonic male before the first six weeks, he, too, would develop into a female.

It was never advisable, when knowing little of these matters, to elaborate any thesis upon them. Who was more to be disrespected than the philosopher who built his system upon scientific conclusions he could not evaluate. How absurd, for instance, were those arguments which would sanctify the power of men by stating that science had shown that the man determined the sex of the child since his sperm contained either male or female chromosomes, and only one or the other would reach the ovum. Caught in such arguments it would appeal to the Prisoner to point out that the scientists who announced such results were hardly bestowing power on the female ovum to call across the diminishing sea, "Here, here, sweet little *x* girl chromosome, come to me," or "Stay where you are, nasty vain ego-swollen *y* sticker chromosome." By such nice logic it seemed evident that the determination of the sex of children was probably as much up to the women

as the men, indeed, even nicer to think that it may
have depended upon the qualities called forth by
the fuck, but he was back again here to the cramped
grasp he held of these ultra-microscopic biological
matters, a cause perhaps of his cynicism about the
power of scientists to state with real certainty that the
sexes were actually as similar in embryo as they might
appear, and that indeed, but for the single different x
or y chromosome, we were all as one sex once. Yet he
believed it anyway, believed the sexes were originally
as one, believed it not on the scientific evidence which
was vastly too scanty, but on the metaphorical feel,
the metaphysical drift, if you will, of his own thought,
which found it reasonable to assume that the primary
quality of man was an assertion, and on the consequence an isolation, that one had to alienate oneself from nature to become a man, step out of nature,
be almost as if opposed to nature, be perhaps directly
opposed to nature, be perhaps even the instrument
of some larger force in that blind goat-kicking lust
which would debase females, make all women cunts,
that being a man was by this extreme sense not even
altogether natural, not if the calm of the seas is seen
as the basic condition of nature, that man was a spirit
of unrest who proceeded to become less masculine
whenever he ceased to strive, that the phallus was

the perfect symbol of man, since no matter how powerful a habit was its full presence, it was the one habit
which was always ready to desert a man. So it would
not have surprised him if the power to be male might
also rest in the power of that just-formed embryo to
pick up some confidence or detestation of the future
from the communicating waves of the womb and the
nutrients offered by the mother, and so could have the
power to embark on the mightiest decision of the life
which was yet to come, the decision to separate oneself
from nature to the extent of becoming a man. Did it
happen on a stroke with no evidence ever of meta-
morphosis from x to y, or of y back to x in the electron
microscope? For, indeed, such theory spoke of the
power to decide not to be male just as well. Yes, such
vision invoked gulfs of choice between the sexes so
great that the surface of man and the surface of women
(which is to say the part of their minds responsive to
tests) would tend to come together in every simulation
of the similar to which civilization had bent their brain,
for equally great was civilized dread at the intellectual
consequences of a concealed but vast difference between men and women.

Of course, such ideas were wild, they were loose,
they would be called lamentable. Yet his aversion remained to the liberal supposition it was good that men

and women become more and more alike; that gave
him a species of aesthetic nausea as subtle and complete as the sense of displacement which comes upon
one in an airplane when it is learned that the sweet
and gentle soul in the next seat is the product of surgi-
cal virtuosities which have extended his life.

Why at this point did he think with admiration of
Millett? Why then of sturdy Millett next to such an
invalid and such an aversion if not for her political
genius in perceiving that any technologizing of the
sexes into twin-unit living teams complete with de-
tachable subunits (kids) might yet have to contend
with the work of D. H. Lawrence. Not, of course, for
any love of children, it would not be until his last
book that one of Lawrence's romances would end with
the heroine pregnant, tranquil, and fulfilled, no, Lawrence's love affairs were more likely to come in like
winds off Wuthering Heights — but never had a male
novelist written more intimately about women —
heart, contradiction, and soul; never had a novelist
loved them more, been so comfortable in the tides of
their sentiment, and so ready to see them murdered.
His work held, on the consequence, huge fascination
for women. Since by the end he was also the sacramental poet of a sacramental act, for he believed nothing human had such significance as the tender majes-

ties of a man and woman fucking with love, he was also the most appalling subversive to the single permissive sexual standard: the orgy, homosexuality, and the inevitable promiscuity attached to a sexual search repelled him, and might yet repel many of the young as they become bored with the similarity of the sexes.

Indeed, which case-hardened guerrilla of Women's Liberation might not shed a private tear at the following passage:

"And if you're in Scotland and I'm in the Midlands, and I can't put my arms round you, and wrap my legs round you, yet I've got something of you. My soul softly flaps in the little pentecost flame with you, like the peace of fucking. We fucked a flame into being. Even the flowers are fucked into being between the sun and the earth. But it's a delicate thing, and takes patience and the long pause.

"So I love chastity now, because it is the peace that comes of fucking. I love being chaste now. I love it as snowdrops love the snow. I love this chastity, which is the pause of peace of our fucking, between us now like a snowdrop of forked white fire. And when the real spring comes, when the drawing together comes, then we can fuck the little flame brilliant and yellow . . ." [10]

Yes, which stout partisan of the Liberation would read such words and not go soft for the memory of some bitter bridge of love they had burned behind. Lawrence was dangerous. So delicate and indestructi-

ble an enemy to the cause of Liberation that to ex-
punge him one would have to look for Millett herself.
If she is more careful with Lawrence than with Miller,
acting less like some literary Molotov, if her disrespect
for quotation is in this place more guarded, if she even
functions as a critic and so gives us a clue to the meaning of Lawrence's life and work, she has become twice
adroit at hiding the real evidence. So she rises from
abuse to those night-school legal briefs — it is crucial
to her case that Lawrence be the "counterrevolutionary sexual politician" she terms him, but since women
love his work, and remember it, she is obliged to bring
in the evidence more or less fairly, and only distort it
by small moves, brief elisions in the quotation, the
suppression of passing contradictions, in short bring in
all the evidence on one side of the case and harangue
the jury but a little further. Since she has a great deal
of evidence, only a careful defense can overthrow her
case. For Lawrence can be hung as a counterrevolutionary sexual politician out of his own words and
speeches. There is a plethora of evidence — in his
worst books. And in all his books there are unmistak-
able tendencies toward the absolute domination of
women by men, mystical worship of the male will, detestation of democracy. There is a stretch in the middle of his work, out in such unread tracts as *Aaron's*

Rod and *Kangaroo,* when the uneasy feeling arrives
that perhaps it was just as well Lawrence died when
he did, for he could have been the literary adviser to
Oswald Mosley about the time Hitler came in, one can
even ingest a comprehension of the appeal of fascism
to Pound and Wyndham Lewis, for the death of nature
lived already in the air of the contract between corporate democracy and technology, and who was then to
know that the marriage of fascism and technology
would be even worse, would accelerate that death.
Still, such fear for the end of Lawrence is superficial.
He was perhaps a great writer, certainly flawed, and
abominably pedestrian in his language when the ducts
of experience burned dry, he was unendurably didactic
then, he was a pill, and at his worst, a humorless nag;
he is pathetic in all those places he suggests that men
should follow the will of a stronger man, a purer man,
a man conceivably not unlike himself, for one senses in
his petulance and in the spoiled airs of his impatient
disdain at what he could not intellectually dominate
that he was a momma's boy, spoiled rotten, and could
not have commanded two infantrymen to follow him,
yet he was still a great writer, for he contained a caul-
dron of boiling opposites — he was on the one hand a
Hitler in a teapot, on the other he was the blessed
breast of tender love, he knew what it was to love a

woman from her hair to her toes, he lived with all the sensibility of a female burning with tender love — and these incompatibles, enough to break a less extraordinary man, were squared in their difficulty by the fact that he had intellectual ambition sufficient to desire the overthrow of European civilization, his themes were nothing if not immense — in *The Plumed Serpent* he would even look to the founding of a new religion based on the virtues of the phallus and the submission of women to the wisdom of that principle. But he was also the son of a miner, he came from hard practical small-minded people, stock descended conceivably from the Druids, but how many centuries had hammered the reductive wisdom of pounds and pennies into the genes? So a part of Lawrence was like a little tobacconist from the English Midlands who would sniff the smoke of his wildest ideas — notions, we may be certain, which ran completely off the end of anybody's word system — and hack out an irritable cough at the intimate intricate knobby knotty contradictions of his ideas when they were embodied in people. For if we can feel how consumed he was by the dictatorial pressure to ram his sentiments into each idiot throat, he never forgets that he is writing novels, and so his ideas cannot simply triumph, they have to be tried and heated and forged, and finally be beaten into shapelessness against the anvil of his profound British skepticism which would not buy his ideas, not outright, for even his own characters seem to wear out in them. Kate Leslie, the heroine of *The Plumed Serpent,* a proud sophisticated Irish lady, falls in love with one of the Mexican leaders of a new party, a new faith, a new ritual, gives herself to the new religion, believes in her submission — but not entirely! At the end she is still attached to the ambivalence of the European mind. Lilly, the hero of *Aaron's Rod,* finally preaches "deep fathomless submission to the heroic soul in a greater man" and the greater man is Lilly, but he is a slim small somewhat ridiculous figure, a bigger man for example strikes him in front of his wife and he is reduced to regaining his breath without showing he is hurt, he is a small hard-shelled nut of contradictions, much like Lawrence himself, but the grandeur of the ideas sound ridiculous in the little cracked shell. Of course, Lawrence was not only trying to sell dictatorial theorems, he was also trying to rid himself of them. We can see by the literary line of his life that he moves from the adoration of his mother in *Sons and Lovers* and from close to literal adoration of the womb in *The Rainbow* to worship of the phallus and the male will in his later books. In fact, Millett can be quoted to good effect, for her criti-

cism is here close to objective, which is to say not totally at odds with the defense:

Aaron's Rod, Kangaroo, and The Plumed Serpent *are rather
neglected novels, and perhaps justly so. They are unques-
tionably strident, and unpleasant for a number of reasons,
principally a rasping protofascist tone, an increasing fond-
ness of force, a personal arrogance, and innumerable racial,
class, and religious bigotries. In these novels one sees how
terribly Lawrence strained after triumph in the "man's
world" of formal politics, war, priestcraft, art and finance.
Thinking of* Lady Chatterley *or the early novels, readers
often equate Lawrence with the personal life which generally concerns the novelist, the relations of men and
women — for whether he played a woman's man or a
man's man, Lawrence was generally doing so before an
audience of women, who found it difficult to associate him
with the public life of male authority. After* Women in
Love, *having solved, or failed to solve, the problem of
mastering the female, Lawrence became more ambitious.
Yet he never failed to take his sexual politics with him,
and with an astonishing consistency of motive, made it the
foundation of all his other social and political beliefs.*

It is fair analysis as far as it goes, but it fails to un-
derline the heroism of his achievement, which is that
he was able finally to leave off his quest for power in
the male world and go back to what he started with, go
back after every bitterness and frustration to his first
knowledge that the physical love of men and women,

insofar as it was untainted by civilization, was the salvation of us all, there was no other. And in fact he had never ceased believing that, he had merely lost hope it could be achieved.

Millett's critical misdemeanor is to conceal the pilgrimage, hide the life, cover over that emotional odyssey which took him from adoration of the woman to outright lust for her murder, then took him back to worship her beauty, even her procreative beauty. Millett avoids the sympathy this might arouse in her female readers (which dead lover is more to be cherished after all than the one who returned at the end?), yes, avoids such huge potential sympathy by two simple critical stratagems; she writes about his last book first, which enables her to end her very long chapter on Lawrence with an analysis of his story, "The Woman Who Rode Away." Since it may be the most savage of his stories and concludes with the ritual sacrifice of a white woman by natives, Millett can close on Lawrence with the comment, "Probably it is the perversion of sexuality into slaughter, indeed, the story's very travesty and denial of sexuality, which accounts for its monstrous, even demented air." Not every female reader will remind herself that Lawrence, having purged his blood of murder, would now go on to write *Lady Chatterley*. But then Millett is not interested in the dialectic by which writers deliver their themes to themselves; she is more interested in hiding the process, and so her second way of concealing how much Lawrence has still to tell us about men and women is simply to distort the complexity of his brain into snarling maxims, take him at his worst and make him even worse, take him at his best and bring pinking shears to his context. Like a true species of literary Mafia, Millett works always for points and the shading of points. If she can't steal a full point, she'll cop a half.

Examples abound, but it is necessary to quote Lawrence in some fullness, a defense of his works rests naturally on presenting him in uninterrupted lines, which indeed will be no hardship to read. Besides, the clearest exposure of the malignant literary habits of the prosecutor is to quote her first and thereby give everyone an opportunity to see how little she shows, how much she ignores, in her desire to steal the verdict.

"You lie there," he orders. She accedes with a "queer obedience" — Lawrence never uses the word female in the novel without prefacing it with the adjectives "weird" or "queer": this is presumably done to persuade the reader that woman is a dim prehistoric creature operating out of primeval impulse. Mellors concedes one kiss on the navel and then gets to business:

"And he had to come into her at once, to enter the peace on earth of that soft quiescent body. It was the moment of pure peace for him, the entry into the body of a woman. She lay still, in a kind of sleep, always in a kind of sleep. The activity, the orgasm was all his, all his; she could strive for herself no more."

This is the passage from which she has drawn her quotation:

"You lie there," he said softly, and he shut the door, so that it was dark, quite dark.

With a queer obedience, she lay down on the blanket. Then she felt the soft, groping, helplessly desirous hand touching her body, feeling for her face. The hand stroked her face softly, softly, with infinite soothing and assurance, and at last there was the soft touch of a kiss on her cheek.

She lay quite still, in a sort of sleep, in a sort of dream. Then she quivered as she felt his hand groping softly, yet with queer thwarted clumsiness among her clothing. Yet the hand knew, too, how to unclothe her where it wanted. He drew down the thin silk sheath, slowly, carefully, right down and over her feet. Then with a quiver of exquisite pleasure he touched the warm soft body, and touched her navel for a moment in a kiss. And he had to come into her at once, to enter the peace on earth of her soft, quiescent body. It was the moment of pure peace for him, the entry into the body of a woman.

She lay still, in a kind of sleep, always in a kind of sleep. The activity, the orgasm was his, all his; she could strive for herself no more. Even the tightness of his arms

143

round her, even the intense movement of his body, and the springing seed in her, was a kind of sleep, from which she did not begin to rouse till he had finished and lay softly panting against her breast.

It is a modest example, but then it is a modest act and Constance Chatterley is exhausted with the deaths of the world she is carrying within — since they will make other kinds of love later, the prosecutor will have cause enough to be further enraged, but the example can show how the tone of Lawrence's prose is poisoned by the acids of inappropriate comment. "Mellors concedes one kiss on the navel and then gets to business." Indeed! Take off your business suit, Comrade Millett.

But it is hardly the time for a recess. We will want to look at another exhibit. The quoted lines up for indictment are from *Women in Love:*

Having begun by informing Ursula he will not love her, as he is interested in going beyond love to "something much more impersonal and harder," he goes on to state his terms: "I've seen plenty of women, I'm sick of seeing them. I want a woman I don't see . . . I don't want your good looks, and I don't want your womanly feelings, and I don't want your thoughts nor opinions nor your ideas." The "new" relationship, while posing as an affirmation of the primal unconscious sexual being, to adopt Lawrence's jargon, is in effect a denial of personality in the woman.

Or is it a denial of personality in Lawrence? Witness how our literary commissar will void the strength of Lawrence's style by cutting off our acquaintance with the marrow of his sensibility, the air of his senses. For Lawrence is always alert to the quiet ringing of the ether, the quick retreat of a mood, the awe of the thought about to be said, then left unsaid, then said after all. But his remarks cannot be chopped out of their setting. A bruised apple at the foot of a tree is another reality from a bruised apple in the frigidaire.

There was silence for some moments.

"No," he said. "It isn't that. Only — if we are going to make a relationship, even of friendship, there must be something final and irrevocable about it."

There was a clang of mistrust and almost anger in his voice. She did not answer. Her heart was too much contracted. She could not have spoken.

Seeing she was not going to reply, he continued, almost bitterly, giving himself away:

"I can't say it is love I have to offer — and it isn't love I want. It is something much more impersonal and harder — and rarer."

There was a silence, out of which she said:

"You mean you don't love me?"

She suffered furiously, saying that.

"Yes, if you like to put it like that. Though perhaps that isn't true. I don't know. At any rate, I don't feel the emotion of love for you — no, and I don't want to. Because it gives out in the last issues . . ."

How different is all this from "going beyond love to 'something much more impersonal and harder,'" how much in fact we have the feeling they are in love.

"If there is no love, what is there?" she cried, almost jeering.

"Something," he said, looking at her, battling with his soul, with all his might.

"What?"

He was silent for a long time, unable to be in communication with her while she was in this state of opposition.

"There is," he said, in a voice of pure abstraction, "a final me which is stark and impersonal and beyond responsibility. So there is a final you, and it is there I would want to meet you — not in the emotional, loving plane — but there beyond, where there is no speech and no terms of agreement. There we are two stark, unknown beings, two utterly strange creatures, I would want to approach you, and you me. And there could be no obligation, because there is no standard for action there, because no understanding has been reaped from that plane. It is quite inhuman — so there can be no calling to book, in any form whatsoever — because one is outside the pale of all that is accepted, and nothing known applies. One can only follow the impulse, taking that which lies in front, and responsible for nothing, asking for nothing, giving nothing, only each taking according to the primal desire."

Ursula listened to this speech, her mind dumb and almost senseless, what he said was so unexpected and so untoward.

"It is just purely selfish," she said.

"If it is pure, yes. But it isn't selfish at all. Because I

don't know *what I want of you. I deliver* myself *over to the unknown, in coming to you, I am without reserves or defenses, stripped entirely, into the unknown. Only there needs the pledge between us, that we will both cast off everything, cast off ourselves even, and cease to be, so that that which is perfectly ourselves can take place in us."*

As we shall soon see, Lawrence will go further than this, he will come to believe that a woman must submit — a most blood-enriching submission, bet on it — yet in that book where such submission takes place, in *The Plumed Serpent* where Kate Leslie has her most profound sex with a man who insists on remaining a stranger and an Indian, the moral emerges that he wants her by the end, wants Kate Leslie just so deeply as she desires him. Lawrence's point, which he refines over and over, is that the deepest messages of sex cannot be heard by taking a stance on the side of the bank, announcing one is in love, and then proceeding to fish in the waters of love with a breadbasket full of ego. No, he is saying again and again, people can win at love only when they are ready to lose everything they bring to it of ego, position, or identity — love is more stern than war — and men and women can survive only if they reach the depths of their own sex down within themselves. They have to deliver themselves "over to the unknown." No more existential statement of love exists, for it is a way of saying we do not know how the love will turn out. What message more odious to the technologist? So Millett will accuse him endlessly of patriarchal male-dominated sex. But the domination of men over women was only a way station on the line of Lawrence's ideas — what he started to say early and ended saying late was that sex could heal, sex was the only nostrum which could heal, all other medicines were part of the lung-scarring smoke of factories and healed nothing, were poison, but sex could heal only when one was without "reserves or defenses." And so men and women received what they deserved of one another. Since Women's Lib has presented itself with the clear difficulty of giving modern woman a full hard efficient ego, Lawrence's ideas could not be more directly in the way. Still, it is painful to think that, quickly as men are losing any sense of fair play, women — if Millett can model for her sex — are utterly without it. Maybe Millett is not so much Molotov as Vishinsky. What a foul exhibit must now be displayed!

Passive as she is, Connie fares better than the heroine of The Plumed Serpent, *from whom Lawrentian man, Don Cipriano, deliberately withdraws as she nears orgasm, in a calculated and sadistic denial of her pleasure:*

148

"By a swift dark instinct, Cipriano drew away
from this in her. When, in their love, it came back
on her, the seething electric female ecstasy, which
knows such spasms of delirium, he recoiled from
her. . . . By a dark and powerful instinct he
drew away from her as soon as this desire rose
again in her, for the white ecstasy of frictional
satisfaction, the throes of Aphrodite of the foam.
She could see that to him, it was repulsive. He
just removed himself, dark and unchangeable,
away from her."

The passage restored will be of interest to any jury
looking for further evidence on the virtues or deter-
rents of the clitoral come:

*She realised, almost with wonder, the death in her of
the Aphrodite of the foam: the seething, frictional, ecstatic
Aphrodite. By a swift dark instinct, Cipriano drew away
from this in her. When, in their love, it came back on
her, the seething electric female ecstasy, which knows such
spasms of delirium, he recoiled from her. It was what she
used to call her "satisfaction." She had loved Joachim for
this, that again, and again, and again he could give her
this orgiastic "satisfaction," in spasms that made her cry
aloud.*

*But Cipriano would not. By a dark and powerful in-
stinct he drew away from her as soon as this desire rose
again in her, for the white ecstasy of frictional satisfaction,
the throes of Aphrodite of the foam. She could see that to
him, it was repulsive. He just removed himself, dark and
unchangeable, away from her.*

And she, as she lay, would realise the worthlessness of this foam-effervescence, its strange externality to her. It seemed to come upon her from without, not from within. And succeeding the first moment of disappointment, when this sort of "satisfaction" was denied her, came the knowledge that she did not really want it, that it was really nauseous to her.

And he, in his dark, hot silence, would bring her back to the new, soft, heavy, hot flow, when she was like a fountain gushing noiseless and with urgent softness from the volcanic deeps. Then she was open to him soft and hot, yet gushing with a noiseless soft power. And there was no such thing as conscious "satisfaction." What happened was dark and untellable. So different from the friction which flares out in circles of phosphorescent ecstasy, to the last wild spasm which utters the involuntary cry, like a death-cry, the final love-cry. This she had known, and known to the end, with Joachim. And now this too was removed from her. What she had with Cipriano was curiously beyond her knowing: so deep and hot and flowing, as it were subterranean. She had to yield before it. She could not grip it into one final spasm of white ecstasy which was like sheer knowing.

And as it was in the love-act, so it was with him. She could not know him. When she tried to know him, something went slack in her, and she had to leave off. She had to let be. She had to leave him, dark and hot and potent, along with the things that are, but are not known. The presence. And the stranger. This he was always to her.

Yes, sex was the presence of grace and the introduction of the stranger into oneself. That was the only medicine for the lividities of the will. So Lawrence would preach, but he was a man in torture. If Millett had wished to get around Lawrence in the easiest way for the advance of the Liberation, she would have done better to have built a monument to him, and a bridge over his work, rather than making the mean calculation she could bury him by meretricious quotation. For Lawrence is an inspiration, but few can do more than respect him on the fly (the way a Soviet official might duck into an Orthodox church to smell the incense). The world has been technologized and technologized twice again in the forty years since his death, the citizens are technologized as well. Who will go looking for the "new, soft, heavy, hot flow," or the "urgent softness from the volcanic deeps" when the air of cities smells of lava, and the mood of the streets is like the bowels turned inside out? What he was asking for had been too hard for him, it is more than hard for us; his life was, yes, a torture, and we draw back in fear, for we would not know how to try to burn by such a light.

Yet, he was a man more beautiful perhaps than we can guess, and it is worth the attempt to try to perceive the logic of his life, for he illumines the passion to be masculine as no other writer, he reminds us of the beauty of desiring to be a man, for he was not much of a man himself, a son despised by his father, beloved of his mother, a boy and young man and prematurely aging writer with the soul of a beautiful woman. It is not only that no other man writes so well about women, but indeed is there a woman who can? Useless for Millett to answer that here is a case of one man commending another man for his ability to understand women — what a vain and pompous assumption, she will hasten to jeer, but such words will be the ground meat of a dull cow. The confidence is that some of Lawrence's passages have a ring — perhaps it is an echo of that great bell which may toll whenever the literary miracle occurs and a writer sets down words to resonate with that sense of peace and proportion it is tempting to call truth. Yet whoever believes that such a leap is not possible across the gap, that a man cannot write of a woman's soul, or a white man of a black man, does not believe in literature itself. So, yes, Lawrence understood women as they had never been understood before, understood them with all the tortured fever of a man who had the soul of a beautiful, imperious, and passionate woman, yet he was locked into the body of a middling male physique, not physically strong, of reasonable good looks, a pleasant to somewhat seedy-looking man, no stud. What a nightmare to balance that soul! to take the man in himself, locked from youth into every need for profound female companionship, a man almost wholly oriented toward the company of women, and attempt to go out into the world of men, indeed even dominate the world of men so that he might find balance. For his mind was possessed of that intolerable masculine pressure to command which develops in sons outrageously beloved by their mothers — to be the equal of a woman at twelve or six or any early age which reaches equilibrium between the will of the son and the will of the mother, strong love to strong love, is all but to guarantee the making of a future tyrant, for the sense of where to find one's inner health has been generated by the early years of that equilibrium — its substitute will not be easy to create in maturity. What can then be large enough to serve as proper balance to a man who was equal to a strong woman in emotional confidence at the age of eight? Hitlers develop out of such balance derived from imbalance, and great generals and great novelists (for what is a novelist but a general who sends his troops across fields of paper?).

So we must conceive then of Lawrence arrogant with mother love and therefore possessed of a mind which did not believe any man on earth had a mind more important than his own. What a responsibility then to bring his message to the world, unique message which might yet save the world! We must conceive of that ego equal already to the will of a strong woman while he was still a child — what long steps had it taken since within the skull! He needed an extraordinary woman for a mate, and he had the luck to find his Frieda. She was an aristocrat and he was a miner's son, she was large and beautiful, she was passionate, and he stole her away from her husband and children — they could set out together to win the world and educate it into ways to live, do that, do all of that out of the exuberance of finding one another.

But she was a strong woman, she was individual, she loved him but she did not worship him. She was independent. If he had been a stronger man, he could perhaps have enjoyed such personal force, but he had become a man by an act of will, he was bone and blood of the classic family stuff out of which homosexuals are made, he had lifted himself out of his natural destiny which was probably to have the sexual life of a woman, had diverted the virility of his brain down into some indispensable minimum of phallic force — no wonder he worshiped the phallus, he above all men knew what an achievement was its rise from the root, its assertion to stand proud on a delicate base. His mother had adored him. Since his first sense of himself

as a male had been in the tender air of her total concern — now, and always, his strength would depend
upon just such outsize admiration. Dominance over
women was not tyranny to him but equality, for dominance was the indispensable elevator which would
raise his phallus to that height from which it might
seek transcendence. And sexual transcendence, some
ecstasy where he could lose his ego for a moment, and
his sense of self and his will, was life to him — he
could not live without sexual transcendence. If he had
had an outrageously unequal development — all fury
to be a man and all the senses of a woman — there was
a direct price to pay: he was not healthy. His lungs
were poor, and he lived with the knowledge that he
would likely have an early death. Each time he failed
to reach a woman, each time he failed particularly to
reach his own woman, he was dying a little. It is hopeless to read his books and try to understand the quirky
changeable fury-ridden relationships of his men and
women without comprehending that Lawrence saw
every serious love affair as fundamental do-or-die: he
knew he literally died a little more each time he missed
transcendence in the act. It was why he saw lust as
hopeless. Lust was meaningless fucking and that was
the privilege of the healthy. He was ill, and his wife

was literally killing him each time she failed to worship his most proud and delicate cock. Which may be why he invariably wrote on the edge of cliché — we speak in simples as experience approaches the enormous, and Lawrence lived with the monumental gloom that his death was already in him, and sex — some transcendental variety of sex — was his only hope, and his wife was too robust to recognize such tragic facts.

By the time of writing *Women in Love*, his view of women would not be far from the sinister. One of the two heroines would succeed in driving her man to his death. His rage against the will of women turns immense, and his bile explodes on the human race, or is it the majority of the races? — these are the years when he will have a character in *Aaron's Rod*, Lilly, his mouthpiece, say:

I can't do with folk who teem by the billion, like the Chinese and Japs and Orientals altogether. Only vermin teem by the billion. Higher types breed slower. I would have loved the Aztecs and the Red Indians. I know they hold the element in life which I am looking for — they had living pride. Not like the flea-bitten Asiatics. Even niggers are better than Asiatics, though they are wallowers. The American races — and the South Sea Islanders — the Marquesans, the Maori blood. That was true blood. It wasn't frightened. All the rest are craven . . .

It is the spleen of a man whose organs are rotting in parts and so, owner of a world-ego, he will see the world rotting in parts.

These are the years when he flirts with homosexuality, but is secretly, we may assume, obsessed with it. For he is still in need of that restorative sex he can no longer find, and since his psyche was originally shaped to be homosexual, homosexuality could yet be his peace. Except it could not, not likely, for his mind could hardly give up the lust to dominate. Homosexuality becomes a double irony — he must now seek to dominate men physically more powerful than himself. The paradoxes of this position result in the book *Aaron's Rod* which is about a male love affair (which never quite takes place) between a big man and a little man. The little man does the housework, plays nursemaid to the big man when he is ill, and ends by dominating him, enough to offer the last speech in the book.

All men say, they want a leader. Then let them in their souls submit to some greater soul than theirs . . . You, Aaron, you too have the need to submit. You, too, have the need livingly to yield to a more heroic soul, to give yourself. You know you have [but] . . . perhaps you'd rather die than yield. And so, die you must. It is your affair.

He has separated the theme from himself and reversed the roles, but he will die rather than yield, even though earlier in the book he was ready to demonstrate that platonic homosexuality saves. It is the clear suggestion that Aaron recovers only because Lilly anoints his naked body, lays on hands after doctors and medicines had failed.

Quickly he uncovered the blond lower body of his patient, and began to rub the abdomen with oil, using a slow, rhythmic, circulating motion, a sort of massage. For a long time he rubbed finely and steadily, then went over the whole of the lower body, mindless, as if in a sort of incantation. He rubbed every speck of the man's lower body — the abdomen, the buttocks, the thighs and knees, down to his feet, rubbed it all warm and glowing with camphorated oil, every bit of it, chafing the toes swiftly, till he was almost exhausted. Then Aaron was covered up again, and Lilly sat down in fatigue to look at his patient.

He saw a change. The spark had come back into the sick eyes, and the faint trace of a smile, faintly luminous, into the face. Aaron was regaining himself. But Lilly said nothing. He watched his patient fall into a proper sleep.

Another of his heroes, Birkin, weeps in strangled tones before the coffin of Gerald. It is an earlier period in Lawrence's years of homosexual temptation; the pain is sharper, the passion is stronger. "He should have loved me," he said. "I offered him." And his wife is repelled, "recoiled aghast from him as he sat . . . making a strange, horrible sound of tears." They are the sickly sounds of a man who feels ready to die in some part of himself because the other man would never yield.

But homosexuality would have been the abdication of Lawrence as a philosopher-king. Conceive how he must have struggled against it! In all those middle years he moves slowly from the man who is sickened because the other did not yield, to the man who will die because he, himself, will not yield. But he is bitter, and with a rage which could burn half the world. It is burning his lungs.

Then it is too late. He is into his last years. He is into the five last years of his dying. He has been a victim of love, and will die for lack of the full depth of a woman's love for him — what a near to infinite love he had needed. So he has never gotten to that place where he could deliver himself to the unknown, be "without reserves or defenses . . . cast off everything . . . and cease to be, so that that which is perfectly ourselves can take place in us," no, he was never able to go that far. By the time he began *Lady Chatterley*, he must have known the fight was done; he had never been able to break out of the trap of his lungs, nor out of the cage of his fashioning. He had burned too many holes in too many organs trying to reach into more manhood than the course of his nerves could carry, he was done; but he was a lover, he wrote *Lady Chatterley*, he forgave, he wrote his way a little further toward death, and sang of the wonders of creation and the glory of men and women in the rut and lovely of a loving fuck.

"When a woman gets absolutely possessed by her own will, her own will set against everything, then it's fearful, and she should be shot at last."
"And shouldn't men be shot at last, if they get possessed by their own will?"
"Ay! — the same!"

The remark is muttered, the gamekeeper rushes on immediately to talk of other matters, but it has been made, Lawrence has closed the circle, the man and the woman are joined, separate and joined.

3

It would be sensible to end our piece. A sentimental toast to Lawrence, a pat on the back to Millett for collecting such prime questions, and a dance around the pole. The value of men has been restored —the beauty of women will serve as balance — mate!

But unhappily the Prisoner is always opening more subjects than he is able to close. If Lawrence ended with dignity and tenderness, it makes it easier to forget that he also lost, he died too early, he had lost, and the thought that men and women kill each other in the years of their love if it is a half-love, or a love drenched with hate, or a love bleak as the resigned air of mates who have become friends, is still pressing the theme. For if it is true, then the mass of men and women murder each other slowly in the years of their living together, or pass on the murder to their children. The fundamental argument of the sexual revolution is still alive to say, "Sex is the search for pleasure by any pit or any hole, and love is your coffin when a family is founded on it."

Yes, the argument was hardly done. If Lawrence had failed, how many could find "the pause of peace of our fucking, between us now like a snowdrop of forked

white fire"? No, as the male and female blurred into a
form which was not yet clearly one, so the center of
preoccupation in sex passed from procreation to the
"soft, warm, wet" of the polymorphous-perverse, from
conception to contraception, from the vagina to the
anus, as if the mark of a civilization dying should be a
mountainous sense of excitement for the hole which
presides over waste. So a trip across the land of Millett
was not all complete. There was homosexuality to sur-
vey, all of the castles, drawbridges, penitentiaries, and
moats at the back door of every heterosexual urge —
the reader might be ready to assume that a look at the
work of Jean Genet is near. But Genet was in no need
of care since Kate Millett had been ready to serve as
his advocate. The quotes of the shyster, for once, were
just. On a consequence, the Prisoner had hardly to use
Genet for more than an occasional example. The real
journey would be through homosexuality itself, and
since that was a subject some were ready to claim was
as large as the hidden half of love, a traveler was
obliged to look for a shortcut. What way more direct
than to take the inquiry through a jail?

Here are two affidavits. They concern the aftermath
of the suppression of a revolt at the Long Island City
Men's House of Detention in New York, 1970, and are
best read against the background of other affidavits not

presented here which speak of prisoners being beaten
with baseball bats.

> *Friday, October 9, 20 or 30 C.O.s came onto my gallery
> and ordered everyone to strip naked. We were then
> marched, hands over heads, into the dayroom. . . . In the
> dayroom I was lined up with about 40–45 other inmates in
> three rows, facing a wall. Deputy warden Ossicow ordered
> us to turn around and face him, saying, "I want to see if
> any of my friends are here."*
>
> *Officer McCoy then said, "Everybody line up, pricks to
> asses. Everyone who gets a hard-on can walk."*
>
> *McCoy then started beating everyone in the back row
> with a club on their buttocks and legs. . . . The physical
> beating was not as painful as the humiliation.*[11]

It is so extraordinary an affidavit, we can be grateful
for corroboration:

> *The evening of October 5, Monday, we were herded into
> the dayroom, naked. A correction officer ordered us to
> stand closer: "I want your dick in the man's ass in front
> of you," he said. "Anyone whose dick gets hard, you walk
> without a beating."* [12]

Still, one account has it on Monday, another on Fri-
day. Unless the event occurred twice, one of the inmates is mistaken, or both convicts made it up. The
Prizewinner was inclined to believe it was too good to
be true but that it could have happened, for only a

policeman or a prison guard was likely to come up with the happy proposition that an erection was equal to physical safety. That could please the paradoxes in a cop's heart. He would (1) offer dispensation, (2) confirm his opinion that criminals were capable of anything, (3) reduce the convicts to helpless younger brothers, and (4) obtain a recharging for the front and back of his pants while watching a free spectacle.

Consider what an implicit statement is offered about the nature of a hard-on, what a recognition that the phallus erect is nothing less than grace under pressure. Here in this naked line of convicts, they would reward any man who was animal enough, insouciant enough, or able to rise above his surroundings. Indeed, they would be rewarding innocence, for only an innocent could assume that the correction officers would not choose to give him a special going-over on the assumption that any man who could get an erection in such a scene had to be the first troublemaker in the House.

It is the middle class which looks upon homosexuality as perversion; the upper classes have kept it as a game reserve, and the working classes, to the degree they live in ghettos and are not part of the middle class, take on homosexuality as a species of poor man's copulation — if the money is not present to sheik a bitch for a night, then a smaller man must do. In a slum, the pecking order is equal to the fucking order. In prison, where the social complexities of sexual choice are reduced, and the natural instinct of punishment is to make inmates feel like units, a man can tell to uncomfortably close measure how much he is a man and how much he is a woman by how many ranks of men could lay their dicks on his ass (we are only using the good language of the forces of law and order) as opposed to how many men have asses which are ready to be laid on. It could be said that just as civil society is founded on money, so prison population is founded on the social holdings of prick-on-ass. The most powerful bugger is the mightiest man. Now, this of course is obviously not to say that every convict in every prison finds his place in a chain of buggery — that is true no more than that all men and women in society decide every attitude by money — but it is certainly to say that buggery is as fundamental to prison as money to social life, and so offers a preview of some aspects of the sexual revolution, or does if sex is currency in the single permissive sexual standard. In fact the paradox of that order to line up phallus to anus, strange phallus on one's own anus, is that it is indiscriminate, nihilistic, disruptive of social order in the prison population, and finally as explosive and degrading to established convict institutions as a brigade of black guerrillas might seem to a Park Avenue apartment house if the tenants were turned out naked and told to dance in a circle — certain apartments had not been yet in the habit of speaking to other apartments, now they were dancing on order from above. It underlines the fundamental dilemma of homosexuality. If a bugger is a man, if he is indeed twice a man — "a male who fucks a male is a double male," says Darling in *Our Lady of the Flowers* — it is because there is no humiliation more profound in prison than to be at the bottom of the order, to be helpless without a protector, and usable as a female by nearly every other convict. One's ass is one's honor in prison. Men commit murder to defend that ass or to revenge it if it has been raped. One's ass becomes one's woman; one's honor is that she is virginal. Just as women will regard themselves as relatively virginal — men may have had them, but not any man, and no man altogether — so most convicts would qualify the conditions under which their ass was relinquished, they would remain relatively virginal, or would try to. The effect of the order to line up against each other indiscriminately was to make them all equally women since it emphasized that the only real phallus in the place belonged to the law. The law could make them obey any coercion, worse, could mock their only conceivable assertion — the man to get a hard-on would be made on the spot an official favorite, would be incorporated temporarily by the law. That is Establishment! It serves to reveal like nothing else the slippery slope on which the prison homosexual tries to live. If by dint of physical strength, courage, determination, even sexual genius, he climbs to a position first among men, an external act can feminize him. There is simply no security for the prison homosexual. Over and over in Genet we are treated to the spectacle of males turning into females. After a few years, Darling, the "double male," is as much female as his mistress Divine, and Adrien Ballon who begins as a stud ends as a queen, ends in fact as Our Lady of the Flowers. At the same time prison females, who usually begin as young boys forced into service by older men or stronger men, spend years trying to work up the slope. In *Miracle of the Rose* we are told: "Only the act of fighting was noble. It was not a matter of knowing how to die but rather how to fight, which is finer." The thought is expanded in a nice description of how a prison female improvises a masculine personality first, then tries to forge a character which might be able to fill it.

Whenever a big shot who was on the war path started heading for me, the fear of blows, physical fear, made me

*back away and double up. It was so natural a movement
that I could never avoid it, but my will made me change
its meaning. Before long I fell into the habit when stepping
back and bending over, of putting my hands on my thighs
or bent knees, in the posture of a man about to dash forward, a posture whose virtue I felt as soon as I assumed it.
I had the necessary vigor and my face became surly. My
posture was no longer due to the jitters but was a tactical
maneuver. . . . Bulkaen, on the other hand, was a little
man whom Mettray had turned into a girl for the use of
the big shots, and all his gestures were the sign of nostalgia
for his plundered, destroyed virility.*

It is worth the reminder that becoming more masculine does not involve simple "imprinting." One has to
dare certain activities which are dangerous and can be
painful. There is nothing automatic about fighting. At
the least one dares profound humiliation. It is no more
easy to become a man than to agree to be a woman.
Indeed, a man can hardly ever assume he has become
a man — in the instant of such complacency he may
be on the way to becoming less masculine. So cultural
conditioning to be masculine or feminine may not be
the arbitrary exercise of a patriarchal society so much
as derive from some instinct or impulse of nature. Determined was the PW to at least consider the possibility that some necessity may exist in human life to rise
above what is easiest and most routine for it, that

humans-with-phalluses, hardly men at birth, must work to become men, not be — as Millett would have it — merely conditioned into men; and humans-with-vaginas, not necessarily devoted from the beginning to maternity, must deepen into a condition which was not female automatically, must take a creative leap into becoming women. If this seemed close to the old strictures of penis envy, he was quick to remind himself that Freud's women were obliged to remain women because attempts to be masculine would fail — whereas he did not know if there was any journey more difficult in a technological world than a woman reaching the deeps of femininity. Certainly it was no easier than for a man to become a hero. Men and women were, after all, equally the inheritors of a male and female personage in their individual psyche, their father and mother no less, and so it might be more comfortable to develop into some middling mix of both sexes. Indeed, in a technological time when the historical tendency was to homogenize the work-and-leisure patterns of men and women (because that made it easier to design the world's oncoming social machine) so a time might arrive which would be relatively free of cultural conditioning, and then males and females might virtually cease to exist. That test where women gave back responses more masculine than the men may have underlined the crisis of civilization more than it disclosed any failure to find the meaning of masculine and feminine, just as the result which demonstrated that heterosexuals could not be distinguished from homosexuals by psychological tests might as well have been stating that all men are homosexual but for their choice not to be: in prison, where such a choice loses social support and is in fact dangerous, it is hardly surprising most of the prison population will be homosexual at one time or another. Indeed the word loses its meaning in jail. They are not homosexual so much as debased males and artificial queers, de-based in the radical meaning of the word — they have been removed from the base impulse to project their semen into the existential center of a woman. If semen was in any way the physical embodiment of a man's vision of a future, then prison shunted his view of the future to the ass: it was society's profoundest way of saying, "You are criminal, and your vision of the future will and must end in shit." "Must" makes the case, for why else should prison reform never succeed in allowing convicts to be alone with their wives or mistresses, when any student of the subject — on the word of a hundred wardens — knows homosexuality is the greatest force for violence in prison. It must be. The males in prison are forever in danger of losing their mas-

culinity, for they do not have even the modest buttresses to the masculine which the outside world
can offer, not a family at dinner or the ability to
bring in money, no exercise of something at which
they are superior (if it is even a hobby) no, just
the existential fact that they are represented by their
phallus rather than their anus, an existential fact
whose statement may be abruptly reversed in any
prison closet. And the queers are enforced queers, they
are not humans-with-phalluses who chose to be female, they have been made female. They are to the
queer outside as the victim of rape to the virgin who
was nicely seduced. So, yes, queers in prison strive to
become part of the male population, and indeed — it
is the irony of homosexuality — try to take on the masculine powers of the man who enters them, even as the
studs, if Genet is our accurate guide, become effemi-
nate over the years. For remind us: homosexuality is
not heterosexuality. There is no conception possible,
no, no inner space, no damnable spongy pool of a
womb. Where a man can become more male and a
woman more female by coming together in the full rigors of the fuck — a sentimental notion to which the
Prizewinner was bound to subscribe — homosexuals, it
can be suggested, tend to pass their qualities over to
one another, for there is no womb to mirror and return

171

what is most forceful or attractive in each of them. So
the male gets more womanly and the queer absorbs
the masculinity of the other — at what peculiar price
literature, not science, will be more likely to inform us.

*During those years of softness when my personality took
all sorts of forms, any male could squeeze my sides with
his walls, could contain me. . . . I longed at the time —
and often went so far as to imagine my body twisting about
the firm, vigorous body of a male — to be embraced by the
calm, splendid stature of a man of stone with sharp angles.
And I was not completely at ease unless I could completely
take his place, take on his qualities, his virtues; when I
imagined I was he, making his gestures, uttering his words:
when I was he. People thought I was seeing double, whereas I was seeing the double of things. I wanted to be myself,
and I was myself when I became a crasher. All burglars
will understand the dignity with which I was arrayed when
I held my jimmy, my "pen." From its weight, material, and
shape, and from its function too, emanated an authority
that made me a man. I had always needed that steel penis
in order to free myself completely from my faggotry, from
my humble attitudes, and to attain the clear simplicity of
manliness.*[13]

Yes, it is the irony of prison life that it is a world
where everything is homosexual and yet nowhere is
the condition of being a feminine male more despised.
It is because one is used, one is a woman without the
power to be female, one is fucked without a womb,

that is to say without awe. For whatever else is in the act, lust, cruelty, the desire to dominate, or whole delights of desire, the result can be no more than a transaction — pleasurable, even all-encompassing, but a transaction — when no hint remains of the awe that a life in these circumstances can be conceived. Heterosexual sex with contraception is become by this logic a form of sexual currency closer to the homosexual than the heterosexual, a clearinghouse for power, a market for psychic power in which the stronger will use the weaker, and the female in the act, whether possessed of a vagina or phallus, will look to ingest or steal the masculine qualities of the dominator. It could even be said that the development of Women's Lib may have run parallel to the promulgation of the Pill. There is a species of male cichlid, a prehistoric fish, who

failed to find the courage to mate unless the female of their species responded with "awe." How one measures "awe" in a fish is a question perhaps better left unanswered, but the implications of this notion that the female's awe of the male is physically necessary to sexual intercourse are surely transparent enough if applied to men and women.[14]

It is Millett at her happiest, pure Left totalitarian. What is more absurd than a man who requires awe? It could be said that a bugger is more absurd since he must depend on weakness in the male before him, whereas a male may require awe of a female to balance the awe he feels for her — if only in some buried domain of the psyche — awe that he dares shoot into the open representative of the great cave of becoming, dares to take on purchase of that immense and fearful existence ringing at the edges of his dreams, that he fucks with some remote possibility of making a child and so is loose in a world where love can no longer be measured by power.

It was then obvious to the Prisoner that he had come to the point where his own curious, even gnomic remarks about the avoidance of contraception would have to be explained, and if he suspected the argument might have to pass over a few more thoughts before revisiting the mysteries of the womb, he was able to console himself with the lone thought that if he was about ready to quote his own work, he must surely be coming to the end of his argument on this unrelenting subject.

IV The Prisoner

OUR READERS ARE HOUSEWIVES, *full time. They're not interested in the broad public issues of the day. They are not interested in national or international affairs. They are only interested in the family and the home . . . Humor? Has to be gentle, they don't*

*get satire. Travel? We have almost completely dropped
it. . . . You just can't write about ideas or broad issues of
the day for women."* [1]

But we are back in the 1950's. Magazine articles
were called "Femininity Begins at Home" and "Have
Babies While You're Young." Some were even called
"Do Women Have to Talk So Much?" or "Cooking Is
Fun to Me!"

*. . . The bored editors of McCall's ran a little article called
"The Mother Who Ran Away." To their amazement it
brought the highest readership of any article they had ever
run. "It was our moment of truth," said a former editor.
"We suddenly realized that all those women at home with
their three and a half children were miserably unhappy."* [2]

It was an era in which men had run women's magazines and run them briskly — if not quite consciously
— toward a totalitarian goal (never to be altogether
achieved) which would look for an American Century.
Since ideological faith depends upon staying inside
the system (because there is no way to treat the chaos
outside) it was a period when women were considered
neurotic if they rebelled against housework. The men
would earn their salary in the tranquillity of equable
labor-management relations and the women would
offer happy homes for the husband's return from the

corporation day — there was a psychiatrist in every suburb. Let a woman show undue panic at the thought of an oncoming hysterectomy, and the surgeon of the psyche (which is to say the doctor of the word) was there to steer a patient to the fact her fear was due to unconscious association: one's past history was going to be removed — that was the fact of the fear. And the American Army would take care of the world. It was an incredible period. Paeans to the American woman, for she "gracefully concedes the top job rungs to men. This wondrous creature also marries younger than ever, bears more babies and looks and acts far more feminine than the 'emancipated' girl of the 1920's or even 30's." [3]

Surely, the Prisoner is not nostalgic for this aurora borealis of the ranch house and the plastic horizon, this insertion of women into a role Betty Friedan will call so tellingly "The Feminine Mystique"; surely all his enthusiasm for the mystery of the womb is not to squeeze women back into that old insane shoe, surely he cannot think that the life of reading "Really a Man's World, Politics" and "What Women Can Learn from Mother Eve" can be preferable to a generation of young women whose adolescence has now passed through Camp, Pop, pot, poot, free poot, LSD, speed, and up the miniskirt, no, nor would he want them to, he is ready to explain that the Feminine Mystique was a tool of still unsophisticated American technologists and totalitarians, that its conception of society was hygienic and anti-sexual, that he hated the Fifties as few men alive, for, if an era could break a man, the Fifties came close to breaking him. Yet it did not feel comfortable to absolve himself. There was a statement he encountered which he could hardly ignore.

The man upholds the nation as the woman upholds the family. The equal rights of women consist in the fact that in the realm of life determined for her by nature, she experiences the high esteem that is her due. Women and men represent two quite different types of being. . . . To one belongs the power of feeling, the power of the soul . . . to the other belongs the strength of vision, the strength of hardness. . . . Reason is dominant in man. He searches, analyzes, and often opens new immeasurable realms. But all things that he approaches merely by reason are subject to change. Feeling in contrast is much more subtle than reason and woman is the feeling and therefore the stable element.

Obviously he did not have to agree that man was there to uphold the nation — his own man was ready to uphold the nation or seek to overthrow it, that would depend on his choice, and on events, and ideally woman would give him strength, but for the rest — he found the language pompous. Yet he could not say he was at war with every remark. Precisely he had been trying to argue that men and women were "different types of being" and with every added tolerance and new sophistication of these months of living with the possibility of the liberation of women, he still felt something like agreement with a balance which would offer men vision and women "the power of the soul."

How disagreeable to admit to himself that the statement was not an editorial in a magazine of the Fifties, nor even a speech ghostwritten for General Eisenhower, that it was not an extract from the philosophy of Lyndon Johnson or Hubert Humphrey, not even banquet remarks by Spiro Agnew. It went past such association. The remarks had appeared in a paper or magazine called the *Frauenbuch,* published in Munich in 1934, and Adolf Hitler had made them — Kate Millett had been ready to offer the quote as proof the writers Miller, Lawrence, and Mailer were sexual reactionaries. Yes, she had certainly been ready. Well, he had come to the conclusion a long time ago that all thought must not cease with Adolf Hitler, that if, in the course of living with a thought, it might appear to run parallel for a time to arguments Nazis had also been near, one should not therefore slam the books, close the inquiry, and cease to think in such direction any further. That would be equivalent to letting the dead Hitler set up barriers on all the intellectual roads which could yet prove interesting and so would be a curious revenge for that Nazism which had been not only a monstrosity and a nightmare, but had also for a few years conquered Europe from within, conquered it before the war, conquered it psychologically. It had been that power to rise up out of chaos and demoralization at a time when other nations were decadent or inert, which had left a residue of political mystery — if there were fifty explanations later, it was hardly until these years of oncoming ecological disaster that it was possible to assume the Nazis may have been a vanguard of the plague who came close to achieving a total technologizing of a state. The confusion was that they had called for a return to traditional, even primitive roots of existence and had indicted the Jews as the whippets of the unisexual, classless future. If Hitler had done more to accelerate such a future than any Jew ever born (since the Second World War had been a centrifuge to drive technology into every reach of social life), his political genius had been to do it in the name of its opposite. Blood has more to tell us than the machine, he was forever telling us as he built the machine. Ever since, it has been intellectually dubious to make any but the most cultivated appeals for a return to the primitive, since Nazi propaganda was always ready to speak in the profoundest tones of instinct and vision and soul even though Hitler would die no more honorably than a junkie addicted to every factory-made pill which could insulate him from blood, instinct, vision, or the oncoming vibrations of his own death.

Still, Millett would never be unready to remind the world of high points in her argument: a Nazi stating, "The Jew has stolen woman from us through the forms of sex democracy. We, the youth, must march out to kill the dragon so that we may again attain the most holy thing in the world, the woman as maid and servant," or Hitler, with his hand dependably in the short hair: "The message of woman's emancipation is a message discovered solely by the Jewish intellect." No, not solely. Never could one say that! Too many fine Wasp ladies would have to be shoved very far aside to give exclusive credit for Woman's Emancipation to the Jews, but was it altogether a wild remark either? The Jews were a spirit of emancipation. The Jewish intellect having once emancipated itself from its own tradition (so filled with awe that old Cabalists had spent their lives daring to learn how to write the name of the Lord, and never dared to pronounce the name because a man who was unholy could shatter the universe at

such an instant: just so primitive had been the Jews)
having freed themselves at the cost of a damage never
measured from the instincts of the Old Hebrew tongue
(so respectful of the rights and powers of trees —
"touch wood!" say the Jews at a proud remark —
that there were eighty-two different words for the
verb to cut: just so primitive had been the Jews) having emancipated themselves (functionally speaking)
from the detestation of a world which would never
trust a people who knew little of the soil, although the
world had barred them from the soil; having overcome
in part their psychic in-bite for sharing the pain of the
well-mannered at an all too successful people who
came out of the ghetto with nervous intricate movements of hands and head and an ineradicable whine of
defeated centuries in the voice (although the well-
mannered had been the first to put them in that
ghetto) yes, the Jews emancipated at last from being
Jews, able to learn the skills of sciences and profes-
sions closed to them for centuries, had of course become the very principle of emancipation. Having lived
for centuries in dread of the vengeance of Satan's mon-
archs on earth (all those gold-bearing Christian kings
and popes!) and in awe before the more intimate
anger of the avenging angels of the Lord, it could be
nobody other than the Jew to race with a speed Gen-

tiles considered unholy through all the accumulated and underemployed lore and culture of Europe, poor and honest people deterred by no distracting greed of the senses after the sensuous penury of ghetto life, none but for the sensuous intoxications of unfettered knock-them-out thought, racing through culture full of private rage at a God who had never forgiven them, who had ground them in His contempt for centuries, no Messiah forthcoming, raced into the technological future full of the incommensurable terror (so deep they might never have intimation of it) that they had excised themselves from the profoundest primitive tradition still alive in Europe — of course the modern Jew, whip-slicked free of taboo, had acquired influence in every field of science, medicine, law, and finance. And technology, like the Jews, was waiting to burst the traditional and cultural restraints which had kept it penned across the centuries. So of course the Jews would be blamed for all the insidious diseases of technology — they were the missionaries for it. Yet it was an excessive guilt to lay, for they were not the first force of technology nor its essential spirit, at most a catalyst accelerating a reaction which had begun in the embryonic hours of Christianity in that moment when Christ was ready to forgive the sons for the sins of the father. No mightier blow had ever been struck against primitive tradition, no idea had ever done so much to encourage men to ignore taboo and experiment with nature. For the fear that sacrilege might now destroy their tribe was removed. Indeed even the adjuration to be brave so that the sons might suffer no curse had been removed. So in the seed of Christianity was an origin of technology, and even conceivably an origin of human mediocrity. The modern Jew had been no more than the last front-runner of the wave, the convert! the modest sweeper of that buried Christian (and now Faustian) vision which would unlock the last mysteries of nature. So Hitler could accelerate German science on lines which followed the inventions of Jews he condemned for being the enemies of a tradition he would himself destroy. It was not so hard to follow. One could also find good Americans who brought freedom to the Vietnamese by liberating forests of mangrove trees from their roots in earth and the populations of hamlets from their bondage in life. So the Prisoner was ready to follow his thought where it would take him — he had no fear he was cousin to a Nazi — no, he was all too emancipated himself — he wished to explore down the alleys of thought the Nazis had come close to shutting forever. Indeed, gifted with a paranoid edge, one could even argue that the Nazis had been the diabolical success of a Devil who wished to cut man off from his primitive instincts and thereby leave us marooned in a plastic maze which could shatter the balance of nature before the warnings were read. No less far could paranoia take you — for what indeed was paranoia but belief in the Devil? He would take his lines of inquiry, then, he would follow his thought where he would.

2

A noble endeavor. What a fall from the heights of this brave impulse, if we are now told the Prisoner proposes to go back to an idea which never fails to irritate, the pure simple idea that masturbation is a vice. Even the archetype of a vice, for it would steal instinct over to the service of psychic control. If that proves irritating, wait! There is a passage in the wings. Why can we tell it is from the land of Millett?

. . . He condemns onanism in the enlightened manner of a Victorian physician: "Masturbation is bad," it "cripples people" and ends in "insanity." Finally outstripping both the Victorians and the Church, Mailer's line would sit well on a Nazi propagandist: "The fact of the matter is that the

prime responsibility of a woman probably is to be on earth long enough to find the best mate possible for herself, and conceive children who will improve the species."

She was quoting from an interview with Paul Krassner of the *Realist,* which the Prizewinner had apologized for reprinting: "In this dialogue, the subjects grind by like boxcars on a two-mile freight." [4]

Q. Do you think you're something of a puritan when it comes to masturbation?

A. I think masturbation is bad.

Q. In relation to heterosexual fulfillment?

A. In relation to everything — orgasm, heterosexuality, to style, to stance, to be able to fight the good fight. I think masturbation cripples people. It doesn't cripple them altogether, but it turns them askew, it sets up a bad and often enduring tension. I mean has anyone ever studied the correlation between cigarette smoking and masturbation? Anybody who spends his adolescence masturbating, generally enters his young manhood with no sense of being a man . . .

Q. Is it possible that you have a totalitarian attitude against [it]?

A. I wouldn't say all people who masturbate are evil, probably I would even say that some of the best people in the world masturbate. But I am saying it's a miserable activity.

Q. Well, we're getting right back now to this notion of absolutes. You know — to somebody, masturbation can be a thing of beauty —

A. To what end? To what end? Who is going to benefit
from it? . . . Masturbation is bombing. It's bombing one-
self. . . .
Q. I think there's a basic flaw in your argument. Why are
you assuming that masturbation is violence unto oneself?
Why is it not pleasure unto oneself? And I'm not defending
masturbation — well, I'm defending masturbation, yes, as a
substitute if and when —
A. All right, look. When you make love, whatever is good
in you or bad in you, goes out into someone else. I mean
this literally. I'm not interested in the biochemistry of it,
the electromagnetism of it, nor in how the psychic waves
are passed back and forth, and what psychic waves are.
All I know is that when one makes love, one changes a
woman slightly and a woman changes you slightly. . . .
If one has the courage to think about every aspect of the
act — I don't mean think mechanically about it, but if one
is able to brood over the act, to dwell on it — then one is
changed *by the act. Even if one has been* jangled *by the*
act. *Because in the act of restoring one's harmony, one has*
to encounter all the reasons one was jangled.
So finally one has had an experience which is nourish-
ing. Nourishing because one's able to feel *one's way into*
more difficult or more precious insights as a result of it.
One's able to live a tougher, more heroic life if one can
digest and absorb the experience.
But, if one masturbates, all that happens is, everything
that's beautiful and good in one, goes up the hand, goes
into the air, is lost. Now what the hell is there to absorb?
One hasn't tested himself. You see, in a way, the hetero-
sexual act lays questions to rest, and makes one able to
build upon a few answers. Whereas if one masturbates, the

ability to contemplate one's experience is disturbed. In-stead, fantasies of power take over and disturb all sleep.

If one has, for example, the image of a beautiful sexy babe in masturbation, one still doesn't know whether one can make love to her in the flesh. All you know is that you can violate her in your brain. *Well, a lot of good that is.*

But if one has fought the good fight or the evil fight and ended with the beautiful sexy dame, then if the experi-ence is good, your life is changed by it; if the experience is not good, one's life is also changed by it, in a less happy way. But at least one knows something of what happened. One has something real to build on.

The ultimate direction of masturbation always has to be insanity.

His thought had been thick — good fights and beau-tiful sexy dames were, alas, the essence of the thick — but he had at least arrived at what he considered a reasonable point: that there was a confrontation be-tween fucking and reality. For the fuck either had a meaning which went to the root of existence, or it did not; sex, finally, could not possess reasonable funds of meaning the way food does. Of course, fucking would not even keep a man alive — by this practical measure it was less meaningful than food. Yet try to decide there is design in the universe, that humans embody a particular Intent, assume just once there is some kind of destiny intended — at the least! — *intended* for us, and therefore human beings are not absurd, not totally absurd, assume some Idea (or at least some clash of Idea versus ideas) is in operation — and then sex cannot comfortably prove absurd. For it is obviously difficult to live with a metaphysics where humans are endowed with design yet the act which makes them is empty of it, more difficult than to assume the design has been given some first sense of what it can become by the character of the presence in which it was made. What a long way of saying good fucks make good babies — the argument would be divinely simple if human perversity did not enter on the instant. But we all know that fucking is thus complex and contradictory that people who can hardly bear each other have sex which is often by mutual consensus sensational, and couples wigged with pot, speed, and the pill fly out on sheer bazazz, "great lovemaking, great!," whereas the nicest love of two fine minds in two fine bodies can come to nothing via fornication — sex is capable of too many a variation, love to some and lust to others! sex can lead to conception and be as rewarding as cold piss — the world is not filled for nothing with people who have faces like cold piss! — sex can be no more than a transaction for passing mutual use, yet heaven can hit your hip; there is no telling, there is never any telling, which is why novelists are forever obsessed with the topic, it is an endless frontier. But such a chartless place! The signposts which pretend to exist are always being reversed: "Masturbation does not lead to insanity, but masturbation does." No, fucking is not a place where one finds one's way. Which is why the urge is powerful to throw up all intellectual work and declare sex absurd, put masturbation in. "Take one's pleasure by any push or pull." But once The Onanist is all the way in, what is to keep the rest of existence, category by outright category, from inching over to the absurd until sexual rights become no more than a tricky species, some half-ass rights to property. But property with no established value at its center is a din of absurd disputes. And conception, if sex is meaningless, is also absurd, at least so long as it remains connected to sex — it is best shunted over to semen banks and the extra-uterine receptacles. Yet conception once liberated from men and women will tend to reduce romantic effort in every other direction, for if the root of one's semen appears to be independent of the virtue of the act, then even fashionable society with its mating rites is an absurd impediment to the quick contribution to human improvement that ideal sperm (preserved by thermostat) can give to ideal ovum. It is a way of guaranteeing that the end game of the absurd is coitus-free conception monitored by the state.

We are dealing with a comic perspective — we hope we are. But since the danger of the absurd is that it proves even more unstable than the search for divine purpose, we may as well explore the possibility sex is meaningful — not to pursue piety — for security's sake. Once again we go to Millett. She is invaluable. Gamblers search all their lives for the kind of bettor who is rarely right in his choices (in order that they may listen carefully before they bet the other side). So she is always present in high focus, out there, pointing the way — with the back of her neck.

Now she is referring to "Womanhood and the Inner Space," by Erik Erikson:

. . . No matter how he tries to brighten the picture, Erikson is incapable of stopping at the right moment, but must always go on to exhibit his own distaste or misgiving for the situation he is trying to reinterpret in such positive terms. Even the possession of a womb becomes a detriment, leaving the female "unfulfilled" every moment she is not pregnant:

> "No doubt also, the very existence of the inner productive space exposes women early to a specific sense of loneliness, to a fear of being left empty or deprived of treasures, of remaining unfulfilled and of drying up. . . . For, as pointed out, clinical observation suggests that in female experience an 'inner space' is at the center of despair even as it is the very center of potential fulfill-

ment. Emptiness is the female form of perdition
— known at times to men of the inner life . . .
but standard experience for all women. To be
left, for her, means to be left empty. . . . Such
hurt can be re-experienced in each menstruation;
it is a crying to heaven in the mourning over a
child; and it becomes a permanent scar in the
menopause."

*To attempt to equate pregnancy with artistic creation (re-
ferred to as a male monopoly of the "inner life") attracts
attention at once, but this is soon lost in the rich prose
picture of menstruation as bereavement. One cannot help
but find the latter an interesting poetic conceit, but essentially absurd as a description of women's emotions. It
might be amusing to pursue Erikson's fancy: by rough
computation, a woman menstruates some 450 times in her
life. One begins to grasp the multiple sorrow of this many
bereavements, that many children she didn't bear, as a
demographer's nightmare.*

What deadly wit! It has all the smart-ass of a class-
room! We can hear students begin to laugh on 450
menstruations; they will come in full on "demographer's nightmare" — menstruation-as-bereavement is
one more part of the absurd. Yet Millett has been nice
enough to give us a clue, in fact, she has given us the
meaning; it is: "to equate pregnancy with artistic creation." For why not begin to think of the ovum as a
specialized production, as even an artistic creation?
Why decide it is inconceivable that somewhere in her

unconscious a woman is able to draw on the essence of her experience and refine a marrow of her emotions, give substance to the force of unrequited desires, and lay in the tendrils of an oath, pull psychic equity out of the pain of her past, and spike the mix with the needle of her spite, that a woman can even search the most isolated ducts of her body for close to every quality she wishes to slip or to fling into the future, can search for what is most artful in her, and maybe will look for what is ill in her as well (since an unhealthy woman might dispose of a quintessential malaise or chasm or rot through a pregnancy she knows will miscarry or go to abort) yes, the present and the past and the notion of a future might all go into the construction of each ovum, even the stupidest and most demoralized of women thereby capable of a physical masterpiece of microscopic creation. If so, consider the woe at its loss each month.

It is a pretty idea, but a simple one, for it does not yet explain the absurdity of repeating the creation 450 times, woe to every bereavement, unless we are ready for the ovum to vary each month — just as the experience of the woman may vary — and also ready to suppose that the most desirable qualities or talents may take months or years of work in the ovaries — what a separate woe if some piece of the work came to fruition after years of experimentation in ovum after ovum and the egg went down the wash like any other, what an intimate pinch to the cramp that month, what a scraping sense of loss — not all bereavements are equal. Now, add some further complexity: that these projects of the months and the years can be over-turned, or put in disorder, or accelerated by sudden new sexual experience, by a fierce fuck which lights a fire, or a splendor of velvet in the night — let us put a German ponderosity on the problem — an *historic* fuck! it has turned the art of the egg into a loveliness and a chaos, even agreeable chaos — she is in love with a new man and he is giving her life, but what woe that particular month, what confusion of woe that (1) she has not conceived with the new and beautiful lover, nor (2) been able to face quite how powerfully the secret center of her ego — not at all in love — is pleased the ovum has missed, and (3) woe, old-fashioned woe, at all the lovely qualities she had pre-pared for making a child in some other scene, with a man, let us say, she did not love; the qualities of the ovum all the more fine and special because she had put more than a normal art into creating a future artist out of her lonely seed, and that was lost. Now with a new lover, other virtues: another kind of child will be pre-pared — he will be an athlete. Or is it an executive who is on the way? What a collision of contradictory and caterwauling woes on such a month!

And other months, other years, which offer no more than a dull grinding week of the curse, horizons everywhere low, no chance of conception. All the springs were filled with the chemicals of contraception. The artwork of the egg is dull and indifferent. Yet the pains grind, for the arts lost to the ovum are now wandering through the body, arts which find no home in the flesh — who will accept the thought that the most unlocatable madness or depression can seep out of the death of such arts? Yes, there is variety enough for 450 separate and crucial bereavements, and if a man is lucky to avoid such intimate confrontation with the failure of his deepest projects each and every month, since he can thereby push on to projects which will take him years, or even blind ten years before he knows how little he has done, it is not a complete gift to his sex. If a woman goes mad out of the pain of coming too close to knowing how much she has left behind, and how much she has lost forever each month, so a man goes mad from knowing too little of why he fails — he is always subject to the pressure of thoughts which cannot reach his brain. Still, who knows what goes into his semen that he may fling across the space of eternity — that few inches of *coitus vaginae* — his measure, his meaning, his vision of a future male. Who knows? His sperm count goes by the million. Are they more than a simple electrical charge, an unrolling of the wave? The ovum is vast by far to the size of the sperm, fifty thousand times larger by volume is the ratio utterly forgotten by his mind — it would hardly matter. The ovum was not so large as the point of a pin, and the sperm would never be seen except as angels — if angels did not mind appearing as newts — dancing by the hundreds and, in a change of field, by thousands in the cold light of the microscope.

Q. I'll tell you what's bugging me — it's your mystical approach. You'll use an expression like, "You may be sending the best baby that's in you out into your hand" — but even when you're having intercourse, how many unused spermatozoa will there be in one ejaculation of semen?
A. Look, America is dominated by a bunch of half-maniacal scientists, men who don't know anything about the act of creation. If science comes along and says there are one million spermatozoa in a discharge, you reason on that basis. That may not be a real basis.
We just don't know what the real is. We just don't know. Of the million spermatozoa, there may be only two or three with any real chance of reaching the ovum; the others are there like a supporting army, or if we're talking of planned parenthood, as a body of the electorate. These sperm go out with no sense at all of being real spermatozoa. They may appear to be real spermatozoa under the microscope,

but after all, a man from Mars who's looking at us through a telescope might think that Communist bureaucrats and FBI men look exactly the same.
Q. Well, they are.
A. Krassner's jab piles up more points. The point is that the scientists don't know what's going on. That meeting of the ovum and the sperm is too mysterious for the laboratory. Even the electron microscope can't measure the striations of passion in a spermatozoon. Or the force of its will.

No, he wasn't interested in the biochemistry of it, nor the electromagnetism of it, nor the answer to such riddles as the meaning of a million sperm, but what he did know was that if sex had meaning, conception could not be empty of it, which was a way, he supposed, of assuming that a woman would hardly conceive equally well with any man. For sex, left to itself, could hardly exhibit less selection than appetite. Biologically, it was difficult, if one began to think on it, to assume a scheme of conception was ready to exist in a female body without all the powers of a scheme of natural contraception as well. Of course, he did not invoke for a moment such barbarities as the rhythm system of the Church, that no more than a torturing of the egg, no, it seemed reasonable to him that among the other biological protections, a woman would have the ability — or had once had the ability — to pick, to

choose, to avoid, even to abort in the early minutes
and first hours of a conception her womb had not desired, and that indeed such a power had once been
formidable, that a woman of other centuries could
have gone through hundreds of menstruations and
thousands of fornications without any great concern
that she would conceive with any man whose sperm
was not superbly suited to the ovum on which she
built her view of how life should be if she were to create it. If there was all of human history to point in
reply that women everywhere conceived in the most
abominable fashion, at the drop of a hat or a handker-
chief, conceived from the trickle of a ridiculous lover
never seen but for one silly night, or conceived in the
middle of a meaningless month, conceived with a
friend or with a stranger equally well, he was ready to
reply that all of woman's subtlety, perversity, bewil-
derment, and hidden critical need was also in the taking of conception, that some women were in an an-
guish to be fertilized — by no matter whom — the egg
had been designed without a man in mind (a pearl of
narcissism had been that egg) and some disruption
more awful even than an undesirable pregnancy was
waiting to seize the body if the creation was once more
squandered — it is lonely women with near to hopeless lives who conceive out of they know not where, a

drunken spill in a hall, a nervous tattoo in the dark, they conceive for the egg, not the semen.

And so as well there must be women who make models of regularity, their ovum brought to standard early, and improved only with the subtlest touches, year after year, women ready to sacrifice any of their ova if the man does not suit the preciosities of their theme — their bereavement slight — women of impeccable neatness, one might assume, and with a husband whose spermatozoa could flail to nowhere for years until she chooses to pick a month to begin a child. Planned parenthood originated in the psyche of many a lady long before contraceptives cruder even than the condom were anywhere near. Yes, through history, there must have been every variation of the power to conceive or not to conceive — it was finally an expression of the character of the woman, perhaps the deepest expression of her character — for that reason a clue to how often she might fall in love; a woman could know love was with her if the power not to conceive had been relinquished on a fine month.

Of course, such power was unconscious; the gift to know why a lover had been taken who made no sense, why he — of all men — should give her a child when others, wild or superbly sensible, had not — that was often beyond her knowledge. The power was unconscious, the power worked at night and in the making of the ovum, the power was no more than an intimation to her mind and therefore not easy to read. She came to mistrust, as men came to hate, the irrational, often intolerable nuisance of a pregnancy in the wrong season, the wrong year, or with the worst mate: there was every pressure to remove this quixotic ability not-to-conceive from the curious values of women, and ship it over to the techniques of men.

Yet, after centuries in which the population of humans increased at the smallest rate, and healthy women only took conception when it was the wisest biological choice in a life sometimes filled with unhappy choices and difficulties, after such centuries with never a contraceptive in sight and women forever out on the existential edge of knowing that to become pregnant might mean their death, yet not to be pregnant might bring on the worst of illness, after such fear-filled and existential centuries, the years of sexual prophylaxis could begin. The birthrate in response began to climb.

Of course, it was medicine which made the difference. Infants did not die with half the frequency that once they did. It was medical technique which kept more people on earth, but also the rate of conception itself may have begun to creep up among even the most sophisticated and civilized of women, for a faculty had been lost. Fortified, stoppered, and staunched with a variety of devices and chemicals which threw their physiology into new places and their sexual heat into intolerable kinks, armed by devices which were infallible, or near-to-infallible, (what an additional anxiety was that!) the power not-to-conceive was now shunted, bewildered, unused, or used in bewildered desperation on odd occasions, a power close to hysteria, for its faculties must have borne resemblance to one of those twitching laboratory rabbits with electrodes planted in the brain.

Yet consider how the loss of such a power would not even compare to the damage done the ovum after years of contraception. What a botched and bewildered half-creation the ovum must become, first dulled by years of atrophy, then pumped up by the abrupt decision to make a child in a planned and particular year. What an incomplete work of female creation! And the woman living no doubt with the fear she had lost the ability to conceive even with semen she did not desire. What a negative eugenics could begin! — what a feverish acceptance of sperm, of any sperm, what legions of the mediocre and the anomalous might yet appear as company for the gorged streams, caked fields, and stricken air of the terminal years — he sometimes wondered if his vision, for lack of some cultivation in the middle, was not too compulsively ready for the apocalyptic.

3

So he turned to look for an education in these matters which might be a little less instinctive than his own. And had the luck to find a paperback which was perfect to his needs, for it was a popularization by a writer named Rorvik of the work of a doctor "internationally known for the discovery and identification of male and female producing sperms," Dr. Shettles, attached to Columbia Presbyterian Medical Center and Associate Professor at the College of Physicians and Surgeons, Dr. Landrum B. Shettles, a name to provoke as much happiness in a novelist as Bella Abzug, for the book associated with the doctor was called *Your Baby's Sex: Now You Can Choose,*[5] and it had worked up a method for determining the sex of a baby — in advance! If the style was precisely what one would anticipate of a discovery announced in the *Reader's Digest,* the book gave at least a clear and simple portrait of the process, and was full of the agreeable vulgarity which ensues when millions of Americans are instructed at once.

During intercourse, the male, on the average, ejaculates 400 million sperm cells into the vagina. Why does the male produce and release so many of these microscopic creatures? Here we do know the answer — or at least part of it. It is because the vaginal environment is so hostile to the sperm cells, which are the smallest cells in the body. They die off by the millions shortly after they are released, slaughtered by the acid that abounds in the vagina.

. . . Taking their size into account . . . the 7-inch journey through the birth canal and womb to the waiting egg is equivalent to a 500-mile upstream swim for a salmon! Yet they often make this hazardous journey in under an hour, more than earning their title as "the most powerful and rapid living creatures on earth."

Only the fittest survive to pass through the cervix into the womb. Here they find a more hospitable environment, more alkaline than acidic. Still, many die along the way; others smash into the back of the womb or go up the wrong Fallopian tube. Many of those that go up the right one will miss the egg anyway, if only by a millionth of an inch.* The idea that the egg exerts some magical power of attraction was disproved under Dr. Shettles' microscope. Those that hit the egg — and there are thousands of them that make it — do so blindly. Soon, though, the egg looks rather like a pincushion, except that in this case the "pins" beat their tails furiously, trying to drill into the egg. That

---

* Rorvik may be pickling the lily.

is a sight never to be forgotten, one that Dr. Shettles calls the "dance of love."

There was a picture in the frontispiece of a black planet with a multitude of wavy lines not unlike pubic hair about its circumference. The caption read:

THE DANCE OF LOVE
THOUSANDS OF SPERM,
LOOKING LIKE PINS IN A PINCUSHION,
FIGHT FOR ADMISSION TO THE EGG'S INNER SANCTUM.
ONLY ONE WILL MAKE IT.

If the sentiments were contestable, the drama was to be nicely drawn.

Under the microscope one can see the sperms making heroic efforts to gain admittance to the egg's inner sanctum, which houses the nucleus and the chromosomes. Many are able to break through the egg's outer core, but only one penetrates the interior, *tail and all, there to merge with the egg's nucleus and create a new human being. As soon as one sperm penetrates the nucleus, all others find the way to the heart of the egg blocked. Some unexplained mechanism . . . renders the innermost portions of the egg absolutely impregnable once it has been fertilized by a single sperm. The egg's unsuccessful "suitors" wear themselves out "pounding at the door" and finally die of exhaustion.*

As you will recall, the sperm carries twenty-three chromosomes and so does the egg. Twenty-two of these

(in each) match up as pairs that determine all the bodily characteristics of the new individual — except for sex. The two remaining chromosomes decide the subject's sex. The female always contributes an X chromosome. If the sperm that penetrates the ovum also carries an X chromosome, the resulting individual will be XX, otherwise known as a girl. But if the sperm carries the Y chromosome, the baby will be XY which, to the geneticist, spells b-o-y.
And that's how Mother Nature does it.

His technical ignorance had proved even more complete than he thought, for one million semen were not as 400 million semen, and there had been no "intervening sea" across which the ovum might call to that x- or y-bearing sperm she was ready to choose. To the contrary, thousands of x and y cells would reach the outer rim of the egg. Still he felt confirmed in his opinion that the woman was as ready to choose the sex of the child as the man. That "outer core," those external regions of the ovum which sperm must first penetrate, were, he must suppose, a cameo of the female, sensitive as any other female flesh to the presence of the man who would enter! Indeed how could the sperm cell fail to force its way with different strength and rhythm if it were an x-bearing female cell, or the male y? The x cells were (as he had just learned) oval and large, the y were round and small. In fact, beneath the light of the phase-contrast microscope, the female sperm cells showed themselves to be sturdy and the male cells quick: the female could survive for days in the Fallopian tubes until the egg was ready to ovulate, but the male cells did not live longer than twenty-four hours and also perished more quickly in the acids of the vagina; this had to imply that a male embryo was the product of timing and speed — only on the day of ovulation could one create a boy. So there was a separate sexual program to be followed for the making of a boy or a girl and this encouraged a metaphysical turn or two on the differences of the sexes, for boys were best conceived when semen was greatest in volume as a result of continence, while female sperm cells always predominated when acts of love had been many and semen was thin. (A man down to his last million sperm could know they were all female.) "Having girls is more fun," said Dr. Shettles. Since he had also discovered that the orgasm of the woman would flush the cervix with alkaline secretions which were kinder than acid to the sperm cell with the y, he recommended that a man in search of a son come after the woman. (By the consequences of this logic, Shettles was also obliged to recommend that the woman have no orgasm if she wished a girl, which opens an expectation of some waves of future ladies conceived in great calm!)

The doctor's methods, followed so religiously as to

take vaginal douches of acid before the act for the making of girls, or alkaline for boys, then employing the most effective coital position (entrance from the rear most likely to start a boy!) would result in success as much as eighty percent of the time. So went his claim. Of course, the argument that the ovum could exercise a choice was not dead. If with every powerful difference between acid and alkali — were the poles of the sexes an electrical distance apart? — with every regard for the separate advantages of male speed or female ability to survive, with every continent safeguarding of testicles to be full of male sperm cells or with bags emptied to Henry Miller's "thin solution of pot cheese," still some powerful fraction resisted determination. The results were eighty percent and not one hundred, and that was only a way of saying the opportunities had increased from five chances in ten to eight out of ten, or by thirty percent. The implication remained that the ovum might still give preference to a rare and most determined male or female cell which had survived the hectic activity or lack of it, the douches, the orgasms, the coital positions, and the hours calculated to wipe it out. The value of reading scientific popularizations is that you could enlarge your vocabulary while retaining your philosophy. He had come through with his ignorance altered, but his argument brought at last to focus, for he knew what he would claim. The first cell of an embryo was put together out of the twenty-three chromosomes of the mother and the twenty-three of the father. Every one of the cells of the human body yet to develop in her womb would contain a replica of those forty-six chromosomes. What a joining was implied, what a sense of union (or what an imbalance!). The essence of one's experience, written on the twenty-three tablets of the chromosomes, would combine with the equal number of the mother. It was as if one nest of hieroglyphics had been put in connection with another, as if two separate languages spoke across a void and then combined into one new and different language. A beautiful and rousing thought, suggestive of the possibility of communication between separate planets or stars, or would be but for the intimate and anguished detail of those thousands of sperm wriggling and pushing and straining through some resistant mass or field, some tissue perhaps of later nightmare — what a sense of awe and exhaustion the sperm must contain, what a fever to continue (he was ready to decide) was the true emotion of the sperm. For it was easier to conceive of that microscopic existence (with its precious cargo of chromosomes) as the heart of some profound emotion, even as the limb of a soul seeking to be born, than to try to believe that this one effort which would succeed out of the myriad of lost efforts was neither rapt nor soulful nor even sensate — just an automatic transfer of cargo. No, one did not want to believe that. It was easier to comprehend a microcosmic universe where the future was delivered with awe from the vaults of the infinitesimal, where the mightiest events were unheard by any order of magnitude in which humans could dwell. Pompous sentiments whose existence he need never endanger by a search for truth, but he liked them nonetheless for their stateliness, even as he swung back to the cynical thought that the ironies of life would shine in the coils of the testes as nicely as anywhere else, and the man who would look to please a woman, or to dominate her by massive repetitions of the act, any stud who would fuck to light a furnace in the ego of his esteem, any fellow in short who would continue to fornicate when he was better advised to fart had drained himself of the little man he wanted to make. The balance of nature had left nothing but balling women in his bags. Which may be perhaps a reason why women love to make love so much — it is their way of guaranteeing that the female of the species will thrive.

But it is not the minute to return to the war of the sexes. There were men after all who wished to have daughters upon occasion, and the Prisoner often thought he was one of them — for that matter, it is possible all of his sperm, male and female, could fly into the vagina with equal passion to reach the egg, there to produce that postcoital state known in middle-class circles as "a wholly satisfying half hour of intercourse." Ah, there is finally a use for a polite word where an obscenity would do, and it is "intercourse," or the running back and forth of streams and races of sensation, evocations beneath our awareness of the senses, it was the kernel of his reason that the unlocking of the orgasm gave a hurl of incandescence or a dim spark of insufficiency to the power of the semen going over the hill, and the semen (whether favored as female or privileged as male) undertook its voyage with the rhythm of that discharging will driven right into the last absurdity of its wriggle, or simply lingered, limp and deadened messenger of an indifferent purpose. And the ovum in its turn would be ready with distaste or desire, ready as any priestess to greet the arcane and dismiss the common, ready as a whore to welcome a wad or get rid of a penniless prick, ready as an empress to find a lord or turn her face to the wall — there was a subterranean war of the will when a man and woman made love and the chance of conception was more than a ghost, then the semen had a life endowed by the coming: male and female sperm passed from their own universe to the other, some to take a leap as brave as the man who sent them out — or an inching to equal his weakness. (Of course there are tyrannical women who desire no more than a worm.) But the orgasm was the mirror of one's existence when conception was not a ghost — every contempt for the timidity of one's life would burn like a scourge on the passage, and every call of the woman for what was magnificent or large as her idea of a future life might pinch the pulse or sour the life of the phallus. But a brave man who could please a proud woman (with an open womb) was returned his bravery and an increase, for the will of a woman had been added to his own. The Prisoner now took his bow. A man might as well swim through seas of feces and sing arias in the dungeons of opprobrium as attempt to write such a sentiment and think he had hope to cop a prize. No thought was so painful as the idea that sex had meaning: for give meaning to sex and one was the prisoner of sex — the more meaning one gave it, the more it assumed, until every failure and misery, every evil of your life, spoke their lines in its light, and every fear of mediocre death. Worse. It was not an age to look for meaning in one's acts — a dread of the future oozed from every leak in the social machine — unless the future could be controlled. That wave of totalitarianism which had begun with the urge to infiltrate the life and control the death of millions had come to close upon every style and habit. Every itch to look at love was being scratched, but the desire to control was beyond any electronic ear in the room, or any recording eye through the wall, now technology bored through the outer cores of pornography and went on to the rim of conception. One could make a boy or a girl if one was ready to swab vinegar or baking soda up one's love, one could so choose to make a boy or a girl if one believed a child begun in the juices of an unencumbered fuck was in no way superior to a baby made with an eye on the alkalinity factor, but such practice was only a toddler's step in those reaches of engineering called genetic, for there was a technology which looked to manipulate the genes of the chromosome — more than one piece of engineering would yet take up squatter's rights in the ovum. The extra-uterine womb, which he had assumed in his innocence was the end of the road, was only the road which led to the theater where they were looking to operate on the Lord, yes, genetic engineering "could conceivably be used in the distant future to create a whole new breed of man — man capable of changing sex after birth and changing it repeatedly." [6]

4

So at last he knew what one found in the land of Millett, yes, that burned-out arid landscape was nothing other than the scientist and the narcissist come together (no narcissist like the oyster!) (no scientist like the clam!), come together to explore the exquisite possibilities of the single permissive sexual standard — a weekend in Beirut as a lady, a gang-bang in Hong Kong as a stud — genetic engineering was on the way. Soon women would acquire the eggs of other women and look to have them fertilized in test tubes by their husband, then, by an operation, *implanted* in their womb. "The woman will carry the child to term and give birth to it just as if it were her own," and that was touching. It was certainly more intimate than adoption (if also suggestive of a schizoid space between the eyes of the embryo). But it was an impractical course because it called for nine months of exploited work in the ranks of the womb-oriented female. Better was such technique when reversed, when "the wealthy woman . . . who wants children but doesn't want to take time out for pregnancy" could have her own egg fertilized by some sperm of her choice, then could "*hire* another woman to undergo implantation and carry the baby to birth for her." [7] Of course, the obvious disadvantage was that this scheme maintained women in a two-class system, and so would encourage the less noble-minded of the Women's Liberationists to become a gestation-free elite. Still, could they live with the shame that their sex would be exploiting its own until the means was found to give wombs to men? Or was it better to ignore the men?

A word from the biologist, Jean Rostand: "It is now a regular thing for perfectly constituted living creatures to be born from a virgin egg without any help from a male, on condition that within the egg there has been produced a doubling of the chromosomes." And the Prisoner learned how it was possible to stimulate the doubling, to trick the egg. If the fry of the fuck had once been a crude and hearty, an ineradicable up-your-daisy which said, at the least, twenty-three chromosomes to your side, twenty-three to mine, now a child would come forth with a wholly symmetrical face, product of a fuck that never had to fail for it came at the head of a pin (which poked the egg into duplicating itself). Conceive of that baby with the symmetrical face: prognosis of sanity — low; narcissism — intact; capacity for incest — infinite.

Yet if his brain was trying to assess these new perspectives, the work had all but been done for him. The point to those mean little waiting rooms in doctors' offices with the prose of *Reader's Digests* in the racks came clear: a new world had been in birth.

Imagine a couple in the year 2000 deciding it is time for another baby. Population problems being what they are, they must first apply for a license to have a child. If the license is granted, they receive a prescription from the appropriate medical authority for a drug that acts as a temporary antidote to the infertility agent that is regularly dumped into the municipal water supply. Then the couple has a number of options open to them. They can take a chance and have a baby "in the old way," simply by having intercourse without any sort of "interference." Or they can use the douche and timing procedures developed by Dr. Shettles in the 1960's, thus greatly increasing their chances of having offspring of the sex they desire. Or, if they don't mind utilizing artificial insemination, they can be guaranteed the sex of their choice by using the "sexing" techniques that Dr. Edwards began applying to humans in the 1970's. Then, there's the diaphragm of the 1980's that lets through sperm cells of only one type. Possibly by this time they may even have access to the pill that determines sex; then if they want a boy, the husband will simply take a blue pill a few hours before intercourse. Or he'll take a pink pill if they want a girl.

Or they could opt for the newest and most exotic technique of all — one that would completely bypass the sexual union of sperm and egg and offer something more than a mere guarantee that the offspring will be of the sex desired. This, of course, is the cloning technique (which will prob-

217

*ably require a special license, above and beyond that re-
quired for more conventional childbirth). Suppose the
couple wants a boy by clonal reproduction. The husband
will then go to his doctor and have several cells removed
from his arm. These will be examined under the microscope, and a particularly healthy-looking one will be
picked out. The doctor will remove the cell's nucleus very
carefully, hold it up to the light, and say, "Congratulations,
here's your baby boy." Then he will remove one of the
wife's egg cells, vaporize its nucleus with radiation from a
laser, and insert the body-cell nucleus in its place. Finally,
he will implant this doctored cell in the wife's uterus . . .
and then let Nature take her course.*

*Nine months later, a baby boy will arrive, and everyone
will have to agree that it is literally "a chip off the old
block." Microscopic studies will show that it is genetically
identical to its "father" in every detail, that it is really
more an identical twin (that arrived several years late)
than a son. As the child grows up, of course, it will look
exactly like its father, which ought to satisfy even the vain-
est of men. If a girl were wanted, the body-cell nucleus
would come from the wife's arm or hand. And would then
be used to "fertilize" her own egg cell, making partheno-
genesis, or "virgin birth," a reality!* [8]

If he had needed a reminder of the thoroughly impractical dispositions of his head, he could think back
to the pep talks he had given to college audiences
when, attempting to draw a portrait of the sexual future upon us in the years of our overpopulation, he

had invoked dreams of the revolutionary commune before which a woman would plead for the right not to
have a compulsory abortion:

WOMAN

You see, brothers, the baby is going to be
beautiful, I know it.

FIRST COMMUNARD

Do you know it, sister? You must tell us how.

WOMAN

Because it came out of the most beautiful
fuck I ever had.

FIRST COMMUNARD

That is what every female comrade will tell
us when she wants a baby. But humankind is
choking the earth — we are obliged to thin
our ranks.

WOMAN

You have a quota for births. I am here to
plead to be a part of that quota.

SECOND COMMUNARD

Is your man with you?

[*The poor fellow steps up and stands modestly before his judges. He is in a state of terror.*]

SECOND COMMUNARD

You, comrade. Do you also want this child?

MAN

[*Cannot speak. Nods.*]

FIRST COMMUNARD

Do you agree it was conceived in the most beautiful fuck of your life?

MAN

It was, brother.

FIRST COMMUNARD

Are you ready to be shot to make room for it?

MAN

I don't know. It may be that I am. I want the child.

THE PRISONER

THIRD COMMUNARD

Hey baby, you got valor.
[*Pronounces it vah-lore. He is Puerto Rican.*]
I say give the comrades permit for the child.

That was a first draft of a future where revolutionary justice would preside. The revised version — he conceived naturally only of the best revolutions — would be more sophisticated.

FIRST COMMUNARD

Say, brother, if you ready to be knocked off
for this child, then you may be looking to cop
your suicide cheap.

SECOND COMMUNARD

You could be a death freak who put a sickly
child into this girl's womb. All that beauty
might have been no more than shit sweet-
talking shit.

MAN

Brothers, if it is the ranks of humans you
wish to reduce, the comrade who made the
last remark may go out in the street with me.
And I will do my best to kill him.

[*A pause for evaluation of this last and extraordinary thought.*]

FIRST COMMUNARD

Sir, you must be King Cunt of the Jivers when it comes to talking heart and soul, but you are also an actor who will take a long chance for a part. So we will allow the child. Its seed is not without its salt.

THIRD COMMUNARD

God bless your revolutionary ass, motherfucker!

Such sentimentality was Dickensian; its worship was excess. (In life, the third Communard was all too likely to be shot.) But he knew that no matter how conservative he became, nor how much he began to believe that the marrows and sinews of creation were locked in the roots of the amputated past, he was still a revolutionary, for conservatism had been destroyed by the corporations of the conservatives, their plastic, their advertising, their technology. Then they had tried to hide the void by marrying themselves to the wrong war. They would inspire no love. Their capture of the future would be a fascistic botch. Yet until one was willing to entrust the rescue of a dying world to the justice of his imaginary court, the other choice was still to submit. Humankind would enter the liberal society of the pink and blue pill.

Of course, the revolution could also become the first bureaucracy of sex, and the technicians of genetics its intelligentsia; at least it could if Women's Lib was Kate Millett — the revolution might be in the years of its final fission between artists and engineers, prophets and programmers, adventurers and technicians, guerrillas and organized echelons of the nonviolent, a way of saying that short of the apocalypse which would explode the technology of us all, you could get ten to one in Las Vegas if you did not think Millett would win. The world would seek solutions where technology was faith and you stayed inside the system. For the violence outside was the violence of the centuries — it lived in the blood and the pores and the genes, it was in the air of every smog. It was in the fear that life had begun to encourage the proliferation of mediocrity it could not afford; and the glutting of the rivers and the caking of the fields was an existential mirror of the greed to buy a piece of security in some environmentally controlled acre where allergy, psychosis, outlaws, echoes of the undead past, and the unmentionable whisper of the north wind could all be endured by the middle registers of the psyche. The passion of the mediocre is to maintain stimulation at its own level. So he had thought it proper to treat Millett with huge attention. If she had not risen any higher on the literary scale than the Upper Mediocre, she was all the more central to the age. She believed in the liberal use of technology for any solution to human pain. So she loathed the forging of the soul in the rigors of paradox, and would never ask an intelligent woman to raise her own child, no, rather she spoke of "the collective professionalization (and consequent improvement) of the care of the young." She had all the technological power of the century in her veins, she was the point of advance for those intellectual forces vastly larger than herself which might look to the liberation of women as the first weapon in the ongoing incarceration of the romantic idea of men — the prose of future prisons was in her tongue, for she saw the differences between men and women as nonessential — excesses of emotion to be conditioned out. So the power of her argument would be greatest for those who wished to live in the modest middles of the poisoned city. She was a way of life for young singles, a species of city-technique. She gave intimation by her presence that the final form of the city was nearer to the dormitory cube with ten million units and the perfect absence of children or dogs. Her superhighway would blast through dread, she was the enemy of sex which might look for beauty at the edge of dread, she would never agree that was where love might go deepest. So she would survive as a force if not a writer, she would be a force to mop up dread — her ideas had been designed to leave spiritual pockets of vacuum which only technology could fill.

5

omewhere in the middle, born out of fatigue and tension and the exhaustion of every lie I had told today, like a gift I did not deserve, that new life began again in me, sweet and perilous and so hard to follow, and I went up with it and leaped and flew over, vaulting down the fall to those washed-out roses washed by the tears of the sea, they washed out to me as my life went in, and I met one cornucopia of flesh and sorrow, scalding sorrow, those wings were in the room, clear and delicate as a noble intent, that sweet presence spoke of the meaning of love for those who had betrayed it, yes I understood the meaning and said, for I knew it now, "I think we have to be good," by which I meant we would have to be brave.

"I know," she said. Then we were silent for a while. "I know," she said again. . . .

I lay there, content to touch the tip of a finger to the tip of a breast, and had that knowledge which falls like rain, *for now I understood that love was not a gift but a vow. Only the brave could live with it for more than a little while. . . . I had had a hint of this before, had it with . . . girls I had known for a night and never knew again — the trains were going in opposite directions. Sometimes with women I had seen for many a month I might have found it on one particular night at the bottom of a barrel of booze. It had always been the same, love was love, one could find it with anyone, one could find it anywhere. It was just that you could never keep it. Not unless you were ready to die for it, dear friend.*

Well, I went back to that embrace with Cherry. We were done, and yet we were not done, for we had a moment when we touched and met the way a bird might light on an evening sea, and we floated off with the tide, deep in each other as the long wash of memory late at night. I could not keep from holding her — had flesh ever promised to forgive me so?[8]

6

till he had not answered the question with which he began. Who finally would do the dishes? And passed in his reading through an Agreement drawn between husband and wife where every piece of housework was divided, and duty-shifts to baby-sit were divided, and weekends where the man worked to compensate the wife for chores of weekday transportation. Shopping was balanced, cooking was split, so was the transportation of children. It was a crystal of a contract bound to serve as model for many another, and began on this high and fundamental premise:

We reject the notion that the work which brings in more money is more valuable. The ability to earn more money is already a privilege which must not be compounded by enabling the larger earner to buy out his / her duties and put the burden on the one who earns less, or on someone hired from outside.

We believe that each member of the family has an equal right to his / her own time, work, value, choices. As long as all duties are performed, each person may use his / her extra time any way he / she chooses. If he / she wants to use it making money, fine. If he / she wants to spend it with spouse, fine. If not, fine.

As parents we believe we must share all responsibility for taking care of our children and home — not only the work, but the responsibility. At least during the first year of this agreement, sharing responsibility shall mean:

1. Dividing the jobs *(see "Job Breakdown" below); and*

2. Dividing the time *(see "Schedule" below) for which each parent is responsible.*

There were details which stung:

10. Cleaning: Husband does all the house-cleaning, in exchange for wife's extra childcare (3:00 to 6:30 daily) and sick care.

11. Laundry: Wife does most home laundry. Husband does all dry cleaning delivery and pick up. Wife strips beds, husband remakes them.[10]

No, he would not be married to such a woman. If he were obliged to have a roommate, he would pick a man. The question had been answered. He could love a woman and she might even sprain her back before a hundred sinks of dishes in a month, but he would not be happy to help her if his work should suffer, no, not unless her work was as valuable as his own. But he was complacent with the importance of respecting his work — what an agony for a man if work were meaningless: then all such rights were lost before a woman. So it was another corollary of Liberation that as technique reduced labor to activities which were often absurd, like punching the buttons on an automatic machine, so did the housework of women take on magnitude, for their work was directed at least to a basic end. And thinking of that Marriage Agreement which was nearly the equal of a legal code, he was reminded of his old campaign for mayor when Breslin and himself had called for New York City to become the fifty-first state and had preached Power to the Neighborhoods and offered the idea that a modern man would do well to live in a small society of his own choosing, in a legally constituted village within the city, or a corporate zone, in a traditional religious park or a revolutionary commune — the value would be to discover which of one's social ideas were able to work. For nothing was more difficult to learn in the modern world. Of course, it had been a scheme with all the profound naïveté of assuming that people voted as an expression of their desire when he had yet to learn the electorate obtained satisfaction by venting their hate. Still he wondered if it was not likely that the politics of government and property would yet begin to alter into the politics of sex. Perhaps he had been living with the subject too closely, but he saw no major reason why one could not await a world — assuming there would be a world — where people would found their politics on the fundamental demands they would make of sex. So might there yet be towns within the city which were homosexual, and whole blocks legally organized for married couples who thought the orgy was ground for the progressive action of the day. And there would be mournful areas of the city deserted on Sunday, all suitable for the mood of masturbators who liked the open air and the street, perhaps even pseudo-Victorian quarters where brothels could again be found. There could be city turfs steaming with the nuances of bisexuals living on top of bisexuals, and funky

tracts for old-fashioned lovers where the man was the
rock of the home; there would always be horizons
blocked by housing projects vast as the legislation
which had gone into the division of household duties
between women and men. There would be every kind
of world in the city, but their laws would be founded
on sex. It was, he supposed, the rationalized end of
that violence which had once existed between men
and women as the crossed potential of their love, violence which was part perhaps of the force to achieve
and the force to scourge, it had been that violence
which entered into all the irrationality of love, "the
rooting out of the old bodily shame" of which Lawrence had spoke, and the rooting out of the fear in
women that they were more violent than their men,
and would betray them, or destroy them in the transcendence of sex; yes, the play of violence had been the
drama of love between a man and a woman, for too
little, and they were friends never to be gripped by
any attraction which could send them far; too much,
and they were ruined, or love was ruined, or they must
degenerate to bully and victim, become no better than
a transmission belt to bring in the violence and injus-
tice of the world outside, bring it in to poison the cow-
ardice of their home. But the violence of lovers was on
its way to disappear in all the other deaths of the prim-

itive which one could anticipate as the human became the human unit — human violence would go to some place outside (like the smog) where it could return to kill them by slow degree — and equally. But he had made his determination on beginning his piece that he would not write of sex and violence too long, for that would oblige him to end in the unnatural position of explaining what he had attempted in other work. So he would step aside by remarking that a look at sex and violence was the proper ground of a novel and he would rather try it there. And content himself now with one last look at his remark that "the prime responsibility of a woman probably is to be on earth long enough to find the best mate for herself, and conceive children who will improve the species." Was it too late now to suggest that in the search for the best mate was concealed the bravery of a woman, for to find the best mate (whatever ugly or brutal or tyrannical or unbalanced or heart-searing son of misery he might appear) was no easy matter but indeed a profound and artistic search for that mysterious fellow of concealed values who would eventually present himself in those twenty-three most special chromosomes able to cut through fashion, tradition, and class.

But now he could comprehend why woman bridled at the thought she must "find the best mate for herself and . . . improve the species." How full of death was the idea if one looked at any scheme which brought people who were fundamentally unattracted to each other down marriage aisles, their qualifications superb, their qualities neuter. So he was grateful to a writer who wrote a book, *The Lady*, published in 1910, Emily James Putnam, first dean of Barnard. She was a writer with a whip of the loveliest wit. He would give the last quotation to her for she had given the hint of a way.

Apart from the crude economic question, the things that most women mean when they speak of "happiness," that is, love and children and the little republic of the home, depend upon the favour of men, and the qualities that win this favour are not in general those that are most useful for other purposes. A girl should not be too intelligent or too good or too highly differentiated in any direction. Like a ready-made garment she should be designed to fit the average man. She should have "just about as much religion as my William likes." The age-long operation of this rule, by which the least strongly individualised women are the most likely to have a chance to transmit their qualities, has given it the air of a natural law.[11]

It was finally obvious. Women must have their rights to a life which would allow them to look for a mate. And there would be no free search until they were liberated. So let woman be what she would, and what she could. Let her cohabit on elephants if she had to, and fuck with Borzoi hounds, let her bed with eight pricks and a whistle, yes, give her freedom and let her burn it, or blow it, or build it to triumph or collapse. Let her conceive her children, and kill them in the womb if she thought they did not have it, let her travel to the moon, write the great American novel, and allow her husband to send her off to work with her lunch pail and a cigar; she could kiss the cooze of forty-one Rockettes in Macy's store window; she could legislate, incarcerate, and wear a uniform; she could die of every male disease, and years of burden was the first, for she might learn that women worked at onerous duties and men worked for egos which were worse than onerous and often insane. So women could have the right to die of men's diseases, yes, and might try to live with men's egos in their own skull case and he would cheer them on their way — would he? Yes, he thought that perhaps they may as well do what they desired if the anger of the centuries was having its say. Finally, he would agree with everything they asked but to quit the womb, for finally a day had to come when women shattered the pearl of their love for pristine and feminine will and found the man, yes that man in the million who could become the point of the seed which would give an egg back to nature, and let the woman return with a babe who came from the root of God's desire to go all the way, wherever was that way. And who was there to know that God was not the greatest lover of them all? The idiocy was to assume the oyster and the clam knew more than the trees and the grass. (Unless dear God was black and half-Jewish and a woman, and small and mean as mother-wit. We will never know until we take the trip. And so saying realized he had been able to end a portentous piece in the soft sweet flesh of parentheses.)

References

CHAPTER II

1. Meredith Tax, "The Woman and Her Mind: The Story of Everyday Life," *Women's Liberation: Notes from the Second Year* (1970), p. 12.
2. Dana Densmore, *Sex Roles and Female Oppression*, a pamphlet (Boston: New England Free Press, n.d.), section IV.
3. Ibid.

237

REFERENCES

4. Martha Shelley, "Commentary," *Off Our Backs* (November 8, 1970), p. 6.
5. Joreen, "The Bitch Manifesto," *Women's Liberation*, p. 5.
6. "Verbal Karate," in *Sisterhood Is Powerful*, p. 558.
7. "Cock Rock: Men Always Seem to End Up on Top," *Rat* (October 29–November 18, 1970), p. 17.
8. Pati Trolander, "Crotch Clawers," *Off Our Backs*, p. 10.
9. Germaine Greer, *The Female Eunuch* (London: MacGibbon & Kee, 1970), publisher's blurb.
10. Ibid., pp. 39, 50–51.
11. Valerie Solanis, "Excerpts from the SCUM (Society for Cutting Up Men) Manifesto," in *Sisterhood Is Powerful*, p. 514.
12. "NOW (National Organization for Women) Bill of Rights," in *Sisterhood Is Powerful*, pp. 513–514.
13. Linda Phelps, *What Is the Difference?*, a pamphlet (3800 McGee, Kansas City, Mo., n.d.), pp. 1–2, 4.
14. Kate Millett, *Sexual Politics* (Garden City, N. Y.: Doubleday, 1970), p. 62.
15. Greer, *Female Eunuch*, pp. 47, 51.
16. Ibid.
17. Densmore, *Sex Roles*, section I.
18. Greer, *Female Eunuch*, p. 48.
19. Lucinda Cisler, "Unfinished Business: Birth Control and Women's Liberation," in *Sisterhood Is Powerful*, p. 264.
20. Densmore, *Sex Roles*.
21. Ti-Grace Atkinson, "The Institution of Sexual Intercourse," *Women's Liberation*, p. 45.
22. Ti-Grace Atkinson, "Radical Feminism," *Women's Liberation*, pp. 33, 36.
23. Mary Jane Sherfey, M.D., "A Theory on Female Sexuality," in *Sisterhood Is Powerful*, pp. 221–222.
24. W. H. Masters as quoted by Dr. Mary Jane Sherfey in "The Evolution and Nature of Female Sexuality in Relation to Psychoanalytic Theory," *Journal of the American Psychoanalytic Association*, vol. 14, no. 1 (New York: International Universities Press, 1966), p. 792, as quoted in Millett, *Sexual Politics*, p. 118.
25. Sherfey, as quoted in Millett, *Sexual Politics*, p. 118.
26. Sherfey, "Theory on Female Sexuality," p. 222.
27. Ibid., pp. 224–225.

28. Frank Caprio, M.D., *The Sexually Adequate Female* (New York: Citadel Press, 1953), p. 78.
29. Anne Koedt, "The Myth of the Vaginal Orgasm," *Women's Liberation*, p. 37ff.
30. Ibid.
31. Ibid.
32. Ibid.
33. Ibid.
34. Sherfey, "Theory on Female Sexuality," p. 228.
35. Greer, *Female Eunuch*, p. 42ff.
36. Ibid., p. 3.
37. Millett, *Sexual Politics*, p. 187.

CHAPTER III

1. Henry Miller, *Tropic of Capricorn* (New York: Grove Press paperback, 1963), p. 30.
2. Henry Miller, *Tropic of Cancer* (New York: Grove Press paperback, 1965), p. 141ff.
3. Henry Miller, *Sexus* (New York: Grove Press paperback, 1965), pp. 180–181.
4. Miller, *Tropic of Capricorn*, pp. 182–183.
5. Dr. Naomi Weisstein, " 'Kinder, Küche, Kirche' as Scientific Law: Psychology Constructs the Female," in *Sisterhood Is Powerful*, p. 212.
6. Ibid., p. 211.
7. I'm afraid this is from Ron Karenga (cf. *Look*, January 7, 1969).
8. Greer, *Female Eunuch*, pp. 25, 28.
9. Ibid.
10. D. H. Lawrence, *Lady Chatterley's Lover* (New York: Grove Press paperback, 1959), pp. 364–365.
11. Donald Leroland, prisoner, quoted by Jack Newfield in the *Village Voice*, December 17, 1970.
12. Richard Flowers, prisoner, quoted by Jack Newfield in the *Village Voice*, December 17, 1970.
13. Jean Genet, *Miracle of the Rose* (New York: Grove Press paperback, 1966), pp. 26–27.
14. Millett, *Sexual Politics*, pp. 209–210.

239

REFERENCES

CHAPTER IV

1. A magazine editor, as quoted by Betty Friedan in *The Feminine Mystique* (New York: Dell paperback, 1970), p. 31.
2. Friedan, *Feminine Mystique*, p. 44.
3. *Look*, October 16, 1956.
4. Norman Mailer, *The Presidential Papers* (New York: Berkley Medallion Edition, 1970), p. 143.
5. David M. Rorvik, *Your Baby's Sex: Now You Can Choose* (New York: Bantam, 1971).
6. Ibid., p. 101.
7. Ibid., p. 83.
8. Ibid., pp. 89–90.
9. Norman Mailer, *An American Dream* (New York: Dial Press, 1965), pp. 163–166.
10. Alix Schulman, "Marriage Agreement," *Off Our Backs*, p. 6.
11. Emily James Putnam, *The Lady* (Chicago: University of Chicago Press, 1970), p. 70.